Beyond Bourdieu

For Phoebe and Vikki

Beyond Bourdieu

From Genetic Structuralism to
Relational Phenomenology

Will Atkinson

polity

First published in 2016 by Polity Press

Polity Press
65 Bridge Street
Cambridge CB2 1UR, UK

Polity Press
350 Main Street
Malden, MA 02148, USA

ISBN-13: 978-1-5095-0748-1
ISBN-13: 978-1-5095-0749-8(pb)

A catalogue record for this book is available from the British Library.

Library of Congress Cataloging-in-Publication Data

Names: Atkinson, Will, 1983- author.
Title: Beyond Bourdieu / Will Atkinson.
Description: Cambridge, UK; Malden, MA : Polity Press, 2016. | Includes
   bibliographical references and index.
Identifiers: LCCN 2016003544| ISBN 9781509507481 (hardback : alk. paper) |
   ISBN 9781509507498 (pbk. : alk. paper)
Subjects: LCSH: Bourdieu, Pierre, 1930–2002. | Sociology.
Classification: LCC HM479.B68 A834 2016 | DDC 301–dc23 LC record
   available at http://lccn.loc.gov/2016003544

Typeset in 11 on 13 pt Sabon
by Toppan Best-set Premedia Limited
Printed and bound in the UK by CPI Group (UK) Ltd, Croydon, CRO 4YY

For further information on Polity, visit our website: www.politybooks.com

Contents

Acknowledgement

Chapter 3 is a revised and lengthened version of an article originally published as 'A Sketch of "Family" as a Field: From Realised Category to Space of Struggle'. *Acta Sociologica*, 57 (3): 221–33. I am grateful to Sage Publications for permission to reproduce this material.

After having of necessity divided things up too much, and abstracted from them, the sociologists must strive to reconstitute the whole. By doing so they will discover rewarding facts. They will also find a way to satisfy the psychologists. The latter are strongly aware of their privileged position; the psychopathologists, in particular, are certain they can study the concrete. All these study, or should observe, the behaviour of total beings, not divided according to their faculties. We must imitate them. The study of the concrete, which is the study of completeness, is possible, more captivating, and more explanatory still in sociology.

Marcel Mauss, *The Gift*
(1954/2002: 103)
Reproduced by permission of Taylor and Francis Books UK

1

Introduction

There is no doubt about it: Pierre Bourdieu is the single most influential sociologist of the later twentieth century. The concepts which made his name – habitus, capital and field, the latter also encompassing his notion of 'the social space' as a national balance sheet of symbolic capital and symbolic power – now, well over a decade after his death, pervade not just his own discipline but the full gamut of social sciences and humanities. Rarely does a month go by, it seems, without a book or article exploring their relevance for this or that subject, or this or that social or intellectual problem. Nor are they any longer confined to their European, let alone French, crucible, finding themselves innovatively applied in research from Shanghai to Chicago and given novel spins as new times and different national contexts demand. Some, especially in the US, have built on Bourdieu's general orientation in his later work to champion an all-purpose 'field theory' (see e.g. Fligstein and McAdam, 2011; Green, 2014; Hilgers and Mangez, 2014), while others, fascinated by the ground-breaking statistical techniques he advocated, have sought to map out the social spaces of their respective nations and their homologies in the manner of *Distinction*, Bourdieu's (1984) *magnum opus* (e.g. Prieur et al., 2008; Rosenlund,

2009). Still more continue to document and elaborate the process through which cultural capital is reproduced over the generations (e.g. Reay, 1998; Lareau, 2003). Numerous scholars, meanwhile, have dedicated almost their entire careers to clarifying, introducing and extending Bourdieu's theoretical tools – no mean feat given their richness, apparent flexibility and dispersion throughout Bourdieu's hefty corpus. In his own terms, then, it seems evident that the spirit and the language of Bourdieu's brand of sociology have come to occupy a somewhat dominant position within the global sociological field, framing research projects and driving debates all across the face of the Earth.

This is not to say the Frenchman is without his critics or doubters, or that all of his concepts have been well understood by even those sympathetic to him. Many, for example, resist his influence on social science on abstract theoretical grounds, if not – since, like Marxism before him, his perspective has been perceived as a threat to the cherished ideals of liberal capitalism – on raw political principle. His theory has been decried as determinist: the habitus, being nothing but an internalization of social structures, was simply another way of painting people as idiotic 'judgemental dopes', to use Harold Garfinkel's famous phrase (Alexander, 1995; Ranciere, 2004). It was depicted as obsessed with social reproduction at the expense of social resistance and change: fields shape habitus, habitus shapes fields, and so the cycle continues forever (Jenkins, 2002). And it was labelled as utilitarian in its view of human beings – we are all seemingly plotting and scheming to maximize our capitals in any field in a purely instrumental manner (Honneth, 1986) – and, at the same time, somewhat overemphatic about the non-conscious, unreflexive, automatic, corporeal nature of practice (Sayer, 2005). Meanwhile even Bourdieu's defenders and appliers have all too often superficially understood and watered down his concepts, combined them with all kinds of antagonistic notions drawn from disparate intellectual sources and subjected them to rounds of critical modification on questionable grounds.

As Bourdieu (1993a, 1997a, 1999a), Wacquant (1993) and others (e.g. Swartz, 1997) frequently lamented, both the enemies and the well-meaning enthusiasts have tended to fall prey to the troublesome *allodoxia* effect – the mistaken reading of one thing as another premised on distance, whether spatial or social, in this instance generated by viewing a body of thought forged in one intellectual field through the lenses and problematics provided by altogether different ones (Bourdieu, 1997a: 451). Hence Bourdieu's theory has often been equated with neo-Marxism, or functionalism, or utilitarianism, and his concepts robbed of their analytical power by being used as little more than fancy synonyms for existing and somewhat vague notions: *habitus* becomes simply another way of saying 'character' or 'self', the label *field* gets applied to any and every social context, group or situation, and *capital* becomes an ornamental alternative to the plain term 'resources'. Worse, as we will see in due course, these supposedly innovative applications can sometimes obscure the pertinent set of generative relations and lead researchers and their readers astray. Ultimately, there has been constant oversight of the fundamental tripartite philosophical core of Bourdieu's vision of the social world from which all his concepts derive their specific meaning and function (in Cassirer's sense): the 'three Rs' of *recognition*, *relationalism* and applied or historicized *rationalism*.

On the first count, linking up with – but giving a much richer sociological architecture for – the latest developments in critical theory pushed by Axel Honneth (1996), the major spring of human action, and thus so many specific quests for capital, is not a cold, calculating, instrumental imperative to maximize profit or reproduce domination, as so many critics, sympathizers and revisers have read into Bourdieu's writings over the years (including Honneth at times), but the highly emotive search for a *reason for being*, generally available in the form of worth and value in the eyes of others. Second, since the desire to attain such recognition *from* others seems inexorably to entail struggle to be seen as worthier *than* others through the imposition of certain arbitrary symbols and properties as legitimate (rendering them *mis*recognized), human beings and their schemes of perception organize around so many systems of difference, dominance and contention vis-à-vis certain definitions of worthiness – i.e. fields – such that any person, practice or property is defined not by some intrinsic essence or substance, as Aristotelian metaphysics had it for centuries, but by their position relative to other people, practices or properties in any one such system. Individual projects and strategies thus flow not from an autonomous cogitator, or *homo clausus* to use Norbert Elias' (1978) phrase, but from a sense of one's place and the possibilities inscribed in it, and resistance, far from being marginalized or absent in Bourdieu's account as some friendly and not-so-friendly critics complain, is endemic. Third, the Frenchman's concepts are rooted in a specifically Gallic tradition of historical epistemology in which systematic reason and the quest for objectivity are only made possible by the development of certain social conditions and in which reality can never be grasped 'as is' but can only ever serve as an *ideal* to be approximated to better and worse degrees (as judged by logic and evidence) through constructed models of the object under investigation. To add two further 'Rs' to the mix, this brand of rationalism thus accommodates a form of *realism*, insofar as the existence of objective social structures shaping and constraining perception is admitted, even if we will never render them other than through approximating models (see further Wacquant, 1989; Vandenberghe, 1999), but also necessitates *reflexivity* on behalf of the researcher, that is, the studied bringing-to-light of one's position in the space of sociological production and the interests and limitations it might impose on intellectual practice.

Bourdieu also spoke of the habitus encompassing a 'dispositional' philosophy of action – which somewhat spoils the Rs theme – but I have made the case elsewhere that, to avoid slipping into determinism and epiphenomenalism, this should be more wholeheartedly rendered using the phenomenology of Edmund Husserl, Maurice Merleau-Ponty and Alfred Schutz (Atkinson, 2010a, 2010b, forthcoming a). On this reading, to put it concisely, the habitus comprises the 'horizons' of perception. This is premised on the phenomenological foundation that conscious experience is bifurcated into a 'theme' and a 'horizon'. The theme refers to whatever conscious attention is focused on, whether they be inner thoughts or objects in the world, though this can be split further into the core (the preponderant focus of attention) and the periphery (that which is within conscious awareness but more marginally so, such as certain background sounds, bodily postures and sensations, etc). The horizon, on the other hand, is all that is automatically co-given in perception without actually being directly presented in the sensual input. This includes an intuition of aspects of a percept not seen (e.g. an object's posterior), or qualities not experienced (e.g. its weight), but also, more importantly, its simultaneous exemplification of multiple classes or 'types' of object, of varying generality, with typical properties, patterns of activity and relations with other objects. Other people are experienced in the same way: when we perceive a person, we automatically attribute subjectivity to them, assume they see us as we see them, and perceive them as exemplars of so many types of person who talk, act and think in typical ways. Anticipation of likely or possible futures, what Husserl dubbed protention, is thus written into the present, co-given with perception of (including inner thought about) an object, subject or event. Often this is experienced as an awareness of 'I can' at the level of motor capacity – something is graspable, climbable, doable, etc., on the basis of protention of one's own corporeal facility and the environment into which it is geared (Merleau-Ponty's 'corporeal schema'). Sometimes, of course, it is experienced as an 'I must', calling out a certain response quasi-automatically – with 'intention-in-action', as Anscombe puts it – but protention also underpins consideration and projection of longer-term goals insofar as certain futures enter thematic consciousness as possible before being stamped with the decisive 'voluntative fiat', to use Schutz's phrase, while others are discounted or, more importantly, never even enter consciousness because they are unthinkable. Tying this back up to relationalism and recognition, however, and going beyond phenomenology by itself, it has to be acknowledged that the typifications and sense of the possible constituting the horizons of perception are rooted in the oppositional stances and labels defining particular fields as well as the conditions of existence provided by possession of capitals within them.

This cluster of philosophical postulates, I believe, offers a fertile basis for investigating the full panoply of human endeavour, and many of the problematic interpretations and uses of the specific conceptual 'tools' they animate stem from their neglect or violation. That argument has sometimes led others to label me an 'orthodox' Bourdieusian, stubbornly unwilling to flout logical foundations for the sake of participating in the race to bestow the label 'capital', 'habitus' or 'field' onto all sorts of social phenomena (e.g. Burke et al., 2013). Yet, in the course of a decade of research on the experience of social class, I have, in fact, come across two troublesome limitations in Bourdieu's *oeuvre*: its inadequacy for making sense of the fullness of mundane, everyday, lived experience (*Erlebnis*) and its insufficiency for making sense of how we each come to be who we are as a whole (*Erfahrung*). For instance, when trying to analyse all the factors playing into people's decisions – to leave school or stay on in education, to undertake vocational courses or academic study, which university to attend and subject to study, which jobs to pursue and so on – as a means of assessing the salience and specific place of class, it quickly became clear to me that there was more going on than seemed to fit neatly into Bourdieu's model of the social space and fields (Atkinson, 2010a, 2010b). Other experiences given by the *time-space location and movement* in the world of not only individuals themselves but the things and people they find about them, for example, clearly contribute to making them who they are and informing their practice, even if locations and movements are, to be sure, shaped in complex ways by struggles within the social space and various fields. When trying to follow this up with a study into the full lived experience and reproduction of class in domestic practice, moreover, it became apparent that many of the routines, struggles, joys and suffering of everyday life and social becoming are, at least in contemporary Western societies, the products of not just one field – not even one as encompassing as the social space – but of relations, balances, tensions and harmonies between a *multitude* of fields vying for attention and desire (Atkinson, forthcoming b).[1] The specific bundles of relations usually put under the labels of *family* and *gender* emerged as two of the most important in this regard.

When I scoured Bourdieu's writings for ways to conceive these phenomena, I found suggestive hints and tips – signposts to pathways not travelled by Bourdieu himself. Yet I also came up against an unsatisfactory insistence that the unit of analysis in any sociological research act should always be a singular field, whether art, law, science or whatever, rather than the contradictory or complementary meshing of a multiplicity of fields in an individual's experience (Bourdieu and Wacquant, 1992: 107). One field should be in the researcher's sights at a time, Bourdieu dictated, or perhaps the articulation of two or more fields – especially when it comes to mapping the place of a particular field of cultural, ideological or economic production within the overarching field of power – and then the relevant habitus and strategies underpinning particular events and artworks/policies/goods can be unravelled. This in turn seemed to be premised on a fundamental epistemological division between 'empirical individuals' – individuals in their full specificity – and 'epistemic individuals' – individuals with only their pertinent properties in relation to a specific field isolated for analysis – and an uncertain assertion, at once a frustrating injunction and an appealing challenge, that the latter are the real subject matter of sociology but that 'conceptual progress' will stem from the invention of concepts and categories able to reconcile individuals as seen in relation to one field with their full concrete specificity (Bourdieu, 1988: 22–3). In one place, tucked away in an endnote, empirical individuality, or 'personality', was even explicitly equated with existence as an agent in multiple fields, making the individual a multifaceted 'social surface', but, once the conclusions for statistical analysis had been considered, this intriguing idea was more or less forgotten, perhaps because, not yet having noticed the multitude of micro-fields structuring everyday life that would crop up in his later works, he saw it as a limited phenomenon (Bourdieu, 2000a: 303n8).

Matters were only made worse when I turned to the writings of others for possible solutions. Many essentially confirm Bourdieu's orientation, including those aiming to rebaptize it as 'field theory' (e.g. Fligstein and McAdam, 2011; Hilgers and Mangez, 2014) and those who believe they are in a position to decree the 'correct' way to do Bourdieusian sociology (e.g. Grenfell, 2010; Swartz, 2013). On the other hand, when I started to pull at the various threads of everyday existence – multiplicity, time-space, gender, family – it soon transpired that many others have expressed considerable dissatisfaction with Bourdieu's treatment of each and either quickly rejected his ideas outright or hastily put forward deeply confused concepts – often a capital of some sort – to fill the supposed blanks. The question of multiplicity, for example, has been raised most persistently and forcefully by Bernard Lahire (1998, 2011) in his programme for a 'sociology of individuals' in France, while Bourdieu's approach to time-space is often said to be undeveloped and, perhaps, in need of a new capital to make sense of differential movement potentials. Allied to this latter argument is a growing discontent among those (Lahire among them) sympathetic to one form or another of network theory – including Norbert Elias' figurational sociology and actor-network theory – who chide Bourdieu for neglecting, or outright dismissing, the intricate chains and webs of interaction, communication and association between people and things situated in concrete time-space. These unquestionably feed into habitus in some way, and field forces surely cannot work without them, yet they are not necessarily neatly bounded or shaped by single fields and, indeed, lack any meaningful conceptual articulation in Bourdieu's work. In recent years, in fact, this has burgeoned into a battle over the very meaning of 'relational sociology' – when we talk about social reality being comprised of bundles of relations, do we mean structural relations as defined by capital distribution, or substantive relations of association and dependence (see e.g. Crossley, 2010; Dépelteau and Powell, 2013; Powell and Dépelteau, 2013)?

As for gender relations and family, feminists and other scholars of intimate life have long been unimpressed by Bourdieu's level of attention to their subject matter and the content of his arguments when he has addressed it. Ambivalence, intersectionality and *resistance* to masculine domination are said to be absent from, or poorly conceived in, his writings, and many have questioned why gender struggles would not constitute a field of their own, or at least a distinct capital. His vision of the family and socialization, despite their centrality to his entire edifice and some fleeting remarks later in his career, is, claim others, too crude to be useful for making sense of how people come to desire what they do and be who they are, requires critical confrontation with psychoanalysis – or the 'psychosocial' – to bring it up to scratch and perhaps, once again, needs to be bolstered by an extra capital capturing familial affect. The 'classic' criticisms that Bourdieu's model of the social world is too determinist, reductionist and reproductionist, and his view of human beings too unreflexive, thus find fertile soil in substantive areas of sociology in which to flower.

In order to answer the research questions I had set myself, and to adequately explain what I uncovered, it was necessary to come to terms with the reservations, modifications and additions launched by others – to work out their logical validity or inconsistency in relation to the philosophical core outlined above. But it was also necessary to devise new concepts and orientations – to ignore Bourdieu's epistemological injunction, in other words, but rise to his challenge and plug the gaps unearthed. In the process, I found, a whole range of fresh research questions and vistas previously neglected by many Bourdieusian sociologists came into view – not by all, to be fair, as there are those out there who have broached similar themes before without following through on their theoretical consequences and for whom, therefore, I might hope (without wanting to coming across as insufferably arrogant) to act as a sort of Lockean conceptual underlabourer. All this is so much as to say that the interventions and elaborations this volume contains are the product of reflections on concrete research problems and findings, and possible starting points for further inquiry, rather than purely theoretical considerations, though I have never been keen on the knee-jerk rejection of careful logical analysis that sometimes gets dressed up as a Bourdieu-style refusal of 'scholasticism' or 'theoreticism'. Rigorous logic, hard won through the development of the scientific field, is and has to be one of the pillars of a historicized rationalism alongside empirical confirmation and confutation.

Phenomenology has been the primary current of inspiration along the way for the simple reason that no other body of thought offers such potential insight into the detail of how we each individually experience the world and come to be who we are. Since other scholars have nudged in this direction too, albeit less surely, it seemed fitting to identify the view of the social world proposed here not as 'genetic structuralism', Bourdieu's own label for his perspective (which has never really taken off despite his influence), but as what Lois McNay (2008) has called 'relational phenomenology'. Within this perspective, the individual's lifeworld as the centre point of multiple, interacting social forces bearing down on experience can become the focal point of analysis, not as a *replacement* for field analysis – which remains essential – but as a *complement* to it. Moreover, the phenomenological constitution of the habitus is, to fit this switch of perspective, pushed a little further than Bourdieu himself went. His depiction of habitus may have been fine for his purposes, but my own research questions have necessitated sharper and more specific conceptual distinctions.

It is in this sense, then, that we can talk of going 'beyond Bourdieu'. It is definitely not a plea to reject Bourdieu's thought outright, nor a claim that his ideas might have been right for their time but have since become outdated, as Archer (2007) would have us believe. Nor am I trying to use his thought as a foil for launching an opposed perspective apparently conquering major problems and partialities of Bourdieu's model – its supposed determinism or objectivism – as is the case with Bruno Latour, whose actor-network theory disavows causal explication in favour of a shallow descriptivism, or Luc Boltanski, whose 'pragmatic sociology of critique' represents a lurch back to voluntarism and subjectivism.[2] Whatever useful points they might flag by-the-by – the underemphasis on materiality within social theory, or the need for greater attention to situational dynamics – such endeavours nearly always rest on gross caricatures for their rhetorical force. Boltanski's (2011) claims that Bourdieu paints people as passive, indoctrinated dupes, for example, somewhat overlooks the resistance and struggle built into the concept of field; his assertion that Bourdieu fails to appreciate the circulation and re-appropriation of sociological knowledge among the populace ignores his long-established idea of the 'theory effect'; and the argument that Bourdieu lacks a philosophical anthropology on which to base his critique of society bizarrely misses the attention Bourdieu paid to recognition, symbolic worth and justification in his later work – all perhaps because Boltanski tries to claim these foci for himself. Yet there is, nevertheless, a need to go past what Bourdieu himself wrote, to take the logic of his thought and apply it in novel ways and to refine it and add in new distinctions and concepts to meet the demands of empirical evidence. This is what I venture to do in what follows.

In the next chapter I tackle the questions of multiplicity, time-space and networks by sketching two conceptual tools complementing the existing Bourdieusian kit: the *lifeworld* and *circuits of symbolic power*. In fact both of these notions exist in embryo in Bourdieu's own writings, but for one reason or another, despite their fruitfulness, he did virtually nothing with them. Chapter 3 then focuses on one of the most important of all fields structuring individual lifeworlds: the family. Another idea present in Bourdieu's work, but left woefully undeveloped, the intention is to lay out the genesis and general features of families as fields, push beyond Bourdieu's own suggestions, demonstrate the concept's capacity to integrate and supersede existing scholarship and open up new avenues for research. Perhaps the major divergence from the letter of Bourdieu's argument is the suggestion that *love* and *care* constitute forms of (mis)recognition and thus symbolic power – or, in short, a capital. Building on this argument I then go on, in chapter 4, to delve into the detail of social becoming – how we develop our dispositions and perceptual schemes, how our desires are directed towards different fields and how these are shaped by the interplay of class, family and schooling. This will involve some engagement with the leading lights of developmental psychology – Piaget, Vygotsky, Freud, Mead – as well as educational research, and the core substantive argument, working up all-too-brief comments by Bourdieu in *Pascalian Meditations* (2000b), will be that struggles for love within the familial field are fundamental to the channelling of the child's libido, and attendant development of competencies and perceptual schemas, towards accumulation of specific 'external' capitals such as economic and cultural capital. Chapter 5 then grapples with the weighty issue of gender, the discussions of family and social becoming having inevitably raised it. While clearing up misunderstandings and defending many of Bourdieu's points against critics, it emerges that only through the lens of relational phenomenology – acknowledging the play of multiple fields and circuits of symbolic power in lifeworlds – do the history, dynamic and lived experience of masculine domination, and feminine resistance, come into sharp relief. The closing epilogue then attempts to distil from the preceding chapters some reflections on the practical possibilities for future research.

2

The Lifeworld

Three missing elements of the everyday

To take a field as the unit of analysis is to start with the social structure and work back to individual experience. The battles, manoeuvres and revolutions within the worlds of politics, law, art, science or whatever, or the broad-scale topology underpinning symbolic domination in any one society, are front stage. Mundane perception and representations of the world, in which being a politician, lawyer, artist, scientist or whatever is only a part of someone's life, must be pushed to one side, therefore, and only a certain 'slice' of each implicated individual – their capital and their dispositions (perceptions, inclinations, desires) in relation to that field alone – isolated for analysis. In the words of Loïc Wacquant, decreeing the appropriate steps of Bourdieu's 'social praxeology' in the text widely regarded as the 'go-to' book on genetic structuralism, the task is to extract only the 'socially efficient resources' for the specific domain of social life under the spotlight, bringing in 'lived experience' solely as it relates to the intuition and articulation of that field's forces – the 'feel for the game', in other words (Bourdieu and Wacquant, 1992: 11). Grenfell (2010: 20) is even more prescriptive. Anyone wishing to do 'proper' Bourdieu-style research must, he asserts, always follow the same three steps: determine the position of the field in question vis-à-vis the overarching field of power, chart the space of positions in relation to the form of recognition at stake in the field, and then map out the habitus individuals have developed by virtue of their position in the field and the strategies which flow from it. Both commentators are, without a doubt, building on statements from the man himself. It was, after all, Bourdieu who firmly declared that 'the true object of social science is not the individual', that 'it is the field which is primary and must be the focus of the research operations' (Bourdieu and Wacquant, 1992: 107), and that people exist for sociology only as 'epistemic individuals' or 'agents', that is, with only a 'finite list of effective properties' distinguished for analysis and all else bracketed out as 'irrelevant' (Bourdieu, 1988: 22–3).

Yet this is not the only way in which sociology inspired by Bourdieu's philosophy can proceed – the 'this way or bust' methodological prescriptions do not follow from the core underlying premises of recognition, relationalism and rationalism. We *can* start with the individual, or a cluster of individuals in a particular sample gathered to illuminate a specific research problem, and attempt to unravel the *total* social structuring of the phenomenology of everyday life and their dispositions as an ensemble. If we do, however, it soon emerges that Bourdieu overlooked, or marginalized, three factors vital to the lived experience of the social world, to the formation of habitus and to the formulation of strategies, each of which has been flagged individually or in combination by others. The first is *multiplicity*, a theme emphasized by a sympathetic critic (or critical sympathizer) in France, Bernard Lahire (1998, 2002, 2011; see also Hillier and Rooksby, 2005). In short, everyday experience, the dispositions and schemes of perception making us who we are, the pains and joys of life and our practices are never wholly structured by a single field, not even one as wide-ranging as the national social space, but by a *combination* of forces – sometimes harmonizing, sometimes clashing – emanating from multiple fields. Obviously this applies to people situated in, say, the political field and the economic field at the same time (a business leader sitting in the UK's House of Lords, for example), but it also brings to the fore all the 'micro-fields', only really acknowledged later in Bourdieu's career (see e.g. Bourdieu, 1998, 2000b, 2005a), in which so many of us are caught up and invested in one way or another, each with their own struggles for particular forms of recognition, dominant and dominated players, doxa, possible moves and so on. Specific firms, organizations, trade unions, schools and prisons are just some examples, though perhaps no micro-field is more significant than the family.[1]

Notions of 'habitus tug' (Ingram, 2011) and 'chameleon habitus' (Abrahams and Ingram, 2013) point roughly in this direction, highlighting that an individual's position and habitus in one field (say, a family) can have an effect on their position and habitus in another (a school, the social space, etc.) and vice versa, and that their interest in each one – their ensnarement in the illusio – may be conspicuously uneven (cf. Costa, forthcoming). Even Bourdieu's (2004a, 2007) own notion of 'cleft habitus' inexorably suggests the significance of multiplicity. At first glance, true enough, it does appear to be something slightly different: he gives the impression his own cleft habitus was born of movement within *one* field, the social space. A deeper analysis, however, paying attention to micro-fields, would doubtless reveal that trajectory to be interwoven with past and ongoing tensions between numerous spaces – family, school, the university world, etc. – all pulling on his desire for recognition. This points to a general limitation in Bourdieu's few analyses of singular individuals, whether Flaubert (Bourdieu, 1996a), Heidegger (Bourdieu, 1990a) or himself (Bourdieu, 2007): they tend to focus on the position and trajectory of an agent in one field and the homology with the social space and the field of power, but many of the smaller-scale struggles for recognition shaping entry into and refracting positions in larger fields are absent or downplayed (cf. Lahire, 2003).

The second element necessary for making full sense of everyday life and formative experience yet muted in Bourdieu's sociology is *time-space*, encompassing the physical location and movement not just of the individual but the objects and entities, including specific other people, constituting the immediate material and social milieu. Bourdieu did not ignore space altogether – his ruminations on the Kabyle house are famous, of course, and later in his career he reflected briefly on the relationship between class and space in contemporary societies too (Bourdieu, 1990b, 1999b). The foundational premise was that all discrete objects and all people, as indivisible corporal entities, occupy a particular *site* in physical space which is, like anything else, defined relationally in terms of its position vis-à-vis all other things and people. Yet even those who are sympathetic to Bourdieu have noted how his sociology of space is, as Savage et al. (2005: 8) put it, 'strikingly underdeveloped' (Bridge, 2004, 2013; Savage, 2011; Bacqué et al., 2015). The focus was invariably on the homologies between physical space and the oppositions of the social world: the arrangement of the Kabyle house and the division of the sexes, for example, or the right bank and left bank of the Seine and economic and cultural capital, or certain housing areas and shopping districts and the dominant and dominated class, and so on. The relationship was, moreover, always generally construed as somewhat one way: spaces and the objects within them become stakes and tools in the struggles of certain fields, being read and appropriated through the interests of the habitus in a field, but do not themselves have any independent effect on habitus, positioning or projects. This is confirmed by otherwise exemplary studies attempting to dissect the homology between social space and physical space outside of France. Both Rosenlund (2009) and Jarness (2013), for example, give the impression that class dispositions and tastes in Norway drive people to live in certain areas or frequent certain shops and cultural venues, but the impacts in return that those specific areas, with their specific houses and residents, and those specific shops, with their specific goods and staff, might have are ignored, presumably being cast as unimportant to the task at hand but also as potential concessions to substantialism. Nor did Bourdieu make much of the fact that neither people nor things stay still. Insofar as movement necessarily takes place in time, this means that – despite his attention to the temporal structuring of consciousness and interest in the imposition of timetables and calendars – he gave scant regard to the entwinement of spatial and temporal ordering.

Yet the material environment, its objects and spaces and the infrastructure of routinized time-space movements and encounters in a social order offer certain 'affordances', i.e. possibilities and impossibilities, and have real effects on experience and, therefore, dispositions and projects (see e.g. Dominguez Rubio and Silva, 2013). Such are the claims, at least, of a clutch of disparate yet influential strands of thought in social science. These include not just those attempting to keep alive the long-standing *interactionist* strain of sociology in which individual action is the product of 'situational' dynamics (Mouzelis, 1995; Collins, 2004; Boltanski, 2011; see also Lahire, 2011), but also those sometimes seen as part of a 'spatial turn' or 'new materialism' in social theory, from Giddens' (1984) structuration theory and Latour's (2005) actor-network theory to Urry's (2007) 'mobility paradigm'. Some allied to the last of these have even gone so far as to claim that, especially in a world of affordable international travel, global awareness and technological development where geographical movement has transformed the nature of societies, an additional capital needs to be added into the mix to fill the void: a 'mobility capital' encapsulating differential capacity to move (Kaufmann, 2002; Kaufmann et al., 2004; Flamm and Kaufmann, 2006; see also Urry, 2007; Ohnmacht et al., 2009).

Of course time-space location and movement of self, others and the objects we find about us are still socially patterned, and not just by the many geographically localized micro-fields we find ourselves in. They are also so many effects of fields which most people experiencing them are *not*

themselves positioned in, including policies from the bureaucratic field (Bourdieu's conception of the state), artefacts and
products from the fields of cultural or economic production,
and images and ideas transmitted by the media field. In the
end Bourdieu seems to lack, therefore, any explicit means of
making sense of what is traditionally called 'system integration', which in Giddens' (1984) formulation can be taken to
mean the specific regulated nexus of spatio-temporal movements, distributions and encounters of people and things
keeping the whole social order going – connecting the people
and position-takings in fields of cultural/ideological/eco-
nomic production and their 'audiences', 'subjects' or 'consumers', in other words.

This brings us to the third element of the everyday and
social becoming said to be neglected by Bourdieu, since it
seems to provide an obvious solution to the puzzle of system
integration while also questioning whether there is not something more to the formation of habitus than the sense
of one's place in a field: social networks (Painter, 2000).
Bourdieu worked with a fruitful and popular notion of social
capital, recognizing that concrete connections and acquaint-
ances can provide a road to recognition, so it would be
absurd to suggest he ignored them completely. Yet the impression he often gave was that interaction and association were
the *effects* rather than shapers of habitus and, underpinning
that, field position. Could that view not be a little too one
way again, as with physical space? Does the web of interactive relations, however they may be read by existing schemes
of perception attuned to field struggles, really have no bearing
on an individual's dispositions and practice? Do our tastes
and desires, our knowledge and projects, not come from
whom we associate with as much as our possession of specific capitals? And are networks – or, if one prefers the
vocabulary of specific theorists, figurations or circuits – not
fundamental to conveying the effects of fields differentially
across time and space? Such are the questions of those who
have recently challenged Bourdieu's claim to 'relational sociology', declaring that causal efficacy, if not primacy, should

be granted to the chains of interactive relations comprising a social order rather than abstract relations of difference vis-à-vis capital (Becker, 2010; Crossley, 2010, 2013; Crossley and Bottero, 2011; DeLanda, 2011: 65).

These, then, are three elements of everyday social experience, each revealing something about the way in which the wider social world is organized, which Bourdieu's own orientation seemed to preclude him from paying much attention to. The strange thing is, however, that Bourdieu does actually provide a couple of concepts which can accommodate these themes and head off the challengers – he just never really developed them since they were secondary to his focus on specific fields. What I want to do here, therefore, is take these lesser-known and under-elaborated ideas and, with the help of some compatible schools of thought – primarily phenomenology, but others too – refashion them into more constructive instruments for rendering the fullness of everyday existence and formative experience, and the circulation of bodies and objects, from a broadly Bourdieusian point of view. In the process, a whole range of novel research problems spring up for investigation. The two concepts are 'habitat' and 'legitimation chains', which will be recast as the *lifeworld* and *circuits of symbolic power* respectively. The first of these is the starting point from which all else will follow.

From habitat to lifeworld

The notion of 'habitat' appears fleetingly in some of Bourdieu's (2013: 141–2) earliest work on Algeria, specifically in relation to the painful disorientation and re-adaption wrought by France's forced 'resettlement' of its colonial subjects. Here it appears to refer to the social organization of everyday, inhabited, material space, particularly domestic space. Later – before the term essentially became synonymous with field position in *Pascalian Meditations* (Bourdieu, 2000b: 152) – Bourdieu (1999b) reflected a little further on the idea, implied now to be the total material environment in which the individual comes to be situated. Being concerned primarily with the homologies between physical space and social space and the multiform struggles to appropriate certain spaces, premised on the primacy of *site*, however, he did not explore how experience, habitus and desire are entwined with movement through space or – any trajectory through space necessarily being a trajectory through time – the specific significance of the temporal structuring of spatial mobility.

As time-geographers have done most to elaborate (see e.g. Hägerstrand, 1975; Pred, 1981a; Thrift, 1996), the passage of any human (or non-human) can be plotted as a path of varying tempo and velocity in three-dimensional geographical space, with the individual's present position being the tip of an ever-advancing 'now line'. This path can, in theory, be a continuous trail across space through time, but we humans are limited by our capacities of physical 'reach', that is, degrees and (given physical barriers) sectors of space which can be traversed in a given time, both corporally and by means of technology, and we are physiologically bound to devote time to sleep and sustenance. These are all so many 'capability constraints'. Not only that, but as Giddens (1984) emphasized in his requisition of time-geography for social theory, humans tend to traverse *routinized* paths in space of varying lengths, repetitiveness and rigidity, retracing the same (or similar) trails at the same (or similar) times. These are (i) facilitated and guided by various 'mobility systems', as Urry (2007) calls them, or interlocking transportation and communication infrastructures; (ii) anchored by various 'stations' – physical spaces acting as hubs, that is, as resting places or sites of sustained activity (though often with their own internal mini-paths and spatial arrangements) which are returned to; and (iii) populated by so many objects, obstacles and other people with their own mappable trajectories. Indeed, insofar as some paths are only enabled by the conjunction or 'coupling' of trajectories in space-time, whether those of people or objects, the complex skein of intersecting time-space routes offer so many 'affordances' and impose so many limits upon what individuals can actually do, 'opening times' or 'trading hours' of shops and businesses being only the most obvious example.

Perhaps, then, a 'habitat' can be reimagined as the totality of the physical and social environment constituted by the individual's routine pathways and stations of varying recurrence and the objects and people commonly encountered along the way, i.e. the spatio-temporal bounds of everyday sensory experience, or, we might say, their *world*. Yet human beings are not simply spatially contained within and propelled through their worlds like objects (*Körper*) but, as living, organic bodies (*Leib*), *inhabit* them, that is to say, they are always-already involved in and engaged with the world, hence making it, to borrow from the phenomenological tradition, a *life*world.[2] A routine time-space path is not, therefore, simply a line in a diagram, but the representation of the comportment of an embodied perceptual field imbued with intentionality (in Husserl's sense) and pursuing a plethora of overlapping projects. Spatial existence is thus experienced not from a *punctum archimedis* but, as Merleau-Ponty (2002) argued, relative to the *body* as the zero-point around which 'here' and 'there', 'up' and 'down', 'left' and 'right' and so on attain their meaning, whilst the experience of time, following a Bourdieusian recasting of Heidegger's reasoning, flows from the projects pursued in the quest for recognition. Importantly, as that human being *qua* perceptual field travels her paths and engages with her world, the stream of experiences meeting her senses leaves a lasting sediment, building a stock of knowledge, or habitus, which then, through the halo of expectations (what is definite, possible, probable or likely given what is known) surrounding perception of phenomena, guides the projection of courses of action within time-space (Schutz, 1972; Husserl, 1992). A 'now line' is, therefore, a graphic representation of the 'biographical situation', to use Schutz's (1970) phrase, or the meeting of history embodied in persons with the manifold histories objectified in all the elements of the world comprising the situation.

'Reach' is, in this way, converted from an objective probability into a subjective sense of traversable and knowable
space, while recurrence of paths, objects and people denotes
degrees of familiarity or, its Schutzian obverse, *anonymity*,
from generic classifications of items and people meeting the
attentive core of consciousness only fleetingly, given by perception of particular symbols ('a computer', 'a police officer'),
to detailed layers of declarative and procedural knowledge,
affective associations and expectations of the frequently seen
and/or used (*my* computer) with their 'quirks', 'places' and
'round-aboutness', as Heidegger had it, or specific people
with whom tracts of time-space are shared. The same process
applies to 'stations'. Indeed, people only use and return to
them, i.e. they only possess their analytical status as stations,
insofar as bare geometric physicality is categorized in the
course of experience, observation and use, with all their
emotional, cognitive and corporeal associations and significances, their various levels of anonymity and their internal
perceptual differentiation and classification – 'buildings',
'shops', 'school', 'dwellings', 'my home', 'my school' and so
on with their own rooms, regions, areas, corners, nooks, etc.
(Bachelard, 1994).

So routine time-space paths, while charted graphically as
trajectories of varying regularity by the analyst, are, for the
being treading them, so many familiar, practical trails packed
with association and expectation dependent upon the
purpose and the experiences usually occurring with them,
incorporated to different degrees dependent upon frequency
and intensity of usage such that the body (sooner or later)
comes to 'know the way' without conscious intervention
(unless something goes wrong). In their totality they spawn
a practical sense of one's 'territory' within the infinite
expanse of the overall spatial universe (Seamon, 1979; Steinbock, 1995). The criss-crossing of multiple paths, meanwhile, become so many more or less typical events and
'encounters' in the Goffmanian sense, loaded with general
and particular significance, shaped by and shaping the individual's perceptual horizons, and what appear as 'coupling

constraints' to the time-geographer are lived as a practical, accreted grasp of what is possible when and with whom ('what is/can be done').

Of course, communication technologies, from the letter to the internet, mean that spatial and temporal co-presence of humans, the actual conjunction of 'now lines', is no longer necessary for the production of encounters, mutual influence and familiarity. Yet those meetings of schemes of perception, even if contemporaneous, are hardly 'outside' of space. They are, rather, enabled by the bridging of two (or more) people's paths by the time-space routes of entities (e.g. paper through the postal service or electrical signals through cables, servers or satellites), and hence, while they may facilitate what Giddens (1984) called 'time-space distanciation', or the increasing global intermeshing of action and experience, they remain dependent upon access along paths to the materials necessary to operationalize those modes of communication. This in turn raises the issue of all those objects encountered in the routine round of time-space activity which *unidirectionally* transmit images, information, ideas, categories and so on emanating from a producer at spatial and/or temporal remove into the individual's world – photographs, books, magazines, newspapers, radio or television programmes, films, the internet via computers or smart phones and such like (cf. Thompson, 1995: 81ff). These too bear upon the stream of consciousness of the individual and thence their typifications, expectations, dispositions and projects, and, insofar as some of their content originates in distant worlds, they are – in tandem with increased chances of interaction given global migratory flows – often claimed to be the source of a supposed new 'cosmopolitanism' (e.g. Beck, 2007). Such declarations, however, often lack a sufficiently nuanced view of the greater or lesser discrepancy between the schemes of perception of the various producers, mediators and receivers and thus the difference between *intended* or assumed meaning/use and the *actual* interpretation and utilization by recipients (cf. Hall, 1980) – a discrepancy which, as both de Certeau (1984) and actor-network theory have demonstrated in their own idiosyncratic ways, extends to *all* human-made objects and spaces, from rooms and streets to microwaves and flower pots (for some examples, see Silva, 2010).

The social structures of the lifeworld

So far, fusing time-geography and phenomenology, we have established that an individual's dispositions and schemes of perception in their fullness are shaped through engagement with their world in its fullness. World and habitus are clearly separable in this account. They are not, as others have implied (e.g. Crossley, 2002: 173), more or less synonymous, even if their entwining is what makes the world a lifeworld, for the routine lifeworld can be departed temporarily for one reason or another, and its constituent elements – spaces, stations, objects, people or timings – can change drastically, generating maladaptation and a sense of foreignness, of being 'out of place', which Bourdieu called 'hysteresis'. The elements of the individual's lifeworld, however, are not random; its objects, stations, spaces, timings, paths and people, and thus the typifications, categories, adaptations, dispositions and projects forged in reply to it, are not haphazardly distributed or 'contingent', as Heller (1984) would have it. Nor, importantly, are they accorded equivalent worth and authority amongst the populace, as if all worlds and dispositions were innocuously 'different but equal'. Instead, the physiognomy of lifeworlds and the values attached to their elements by both the subject at the centre and others co-experiencing the same objects from their own vantage point are shaped by the intermeshing effects of so many social structures – a fact that mainstream phenomenology has, of course, famously struggled (or refused) to grasp.

To be more precise – and undergirding the time-geographers' focus on 'authority constraints', which speak implicitly of symbolic power (Pred, 1977, 1981b) – every element within one's lived world, and thus the adaptations to it and projects pursued within it, are, returning to Bourdieu, artefacts, or 'instantiations' to use Giddens' (1984) term, of relatively autonomous *systems of relations of difference and domination* – social spaces and fields, in other words – which, whilst separable from and transcending physical space, possess topologies of their own. These are, as Bourdieu himself would put it, the conditions of possibility of lifeworld experience (Bourdieu and Wacquant, 1992: 73; Bourdieu, 2002), yet when approached from this angle – from the lifeworld as point of departure rather than a single field – not only do the elements of everyday life missed by Bourdieu come into view, but they force us to nuance our understanding of how fields work.

Multiplicity

First of all, *multiplicity*, and with it a range of insights sidelined by Bourdieu but of profound significance for understanding the privations and pains of everyday life and how routine practice actually unfolds, comes centre stage. An object, person or event, for example, can have significance in relation to more than one field at a time for an individual, or *multiple pertinences*. A conference plenary, for example, may bolster one's capital in the intellectual field, but the time away diminishes affective recognition in the familial microcosm, or competes with the kind of tasks bringing administrative power in one's employing institution understood as a field of struggle.[3] They may also prompt actions and projects constituting components of strategies in more than one field, or *multiple plays* – for example, offering to bring a partner and children to the conference site for a vacation (which may backfire if too much time is then spent at the conference).[4] Doxic knowledge and perception from each field, moreover, will be shared with different people encountered in the lifeworld, giving rise to *multiple and incommensurable sources of intersubjectivity*. These may be more or less bounded in time-space, as experiences comprising field determinations are associated with different stations, but – especially in a world of smart phones, ever-present email and so on – never perfectly so. Imagine the different shared understandings drawn on, for instance, when switching between talking to one's partner and a colleague when sharing a lift in a hotel near the conference, both of whom may only be able to read each other on the basis of mutual participation in the general social and symbolic spaces. Finally, if the habitus comprises the horizons of experience, fringing all present perception with a sense of potentialities, then it has to be recognized that perception and practice in relation to one field *necessarily has in its horizons the present and potential state of play in other fields* and, thus, what may occur in them as a result – anticipating that going solo to the conference may diminish affective recognition, for example. We might call this, after Husserl, the 'world horizon'. Fields are only ever *relatively* autonomous from one another, after all, and this is just one banal way – never mind the more marked instances of the logic of one field (e.g. economic) invading that of another (e.g. intellectual) – in which that relativity is constantly manifest in practice.

The articulation, conflict, tension, balance of investment (i.e. which fields one feels a stronger pull towards and why) and flow of the stream of attentive consciousness between fields, as well as the time-space structuring and – successful or not – management of their demands in the routine lifeworld thus all emerge blinking and bleary-eyed into the sociological light. So too do the impacts of historical trends in relations between fields for everyday lives, struggles and practices, including feminization of the workforce (cf. McNay, 1999), concerns over 'long hours culture' and 'work–life balance' (and its toll on mental health), the circulation of the capital rich between numerous fields within the field of power and so on. The notion of *social surface* – encompassing the totality of the individual's dispositions across myriad fields, the habitus *in toto* as opposed to the habitus in relation to just one specific field, fastened together by the world horizon – is therefore no mere side-concept, as Bourdieu thought it to be, but pivotal to comprehending the pains and pleasures of contemporary human existence. This is not, however, the same as Lahire's (2011) overly divided

'plural actor', premised on a perfunctory dismissal of phenomenology, or the postmodern declarations of 'fragmented'
identities (e.g. Jameson, 1991), since, while there are multiple
fields (and thus doxai, positions and capitals) shaping an
individual's world, and while these may well be contradictory and clashing, they still logically aggregate – except in
extreme cases of psychiatric disorder – to furnish an overall
unitary phenomenological sense of 'my world', 'my territory',
'my life' and so on.

The dialectic of fields with space and networks

Second, fusing time-geography and phenomenology with
Bourdieu's vision of social structures yields a more nuanced
treatment of the relationship between the abstract relations
of social spaces and concrete objects, spaces and encounters.
In short, we can see that it is no mere one-way determinism but, instead, *dialectical*. Other scholars have suggested
as much, though usually in a less than satisfactory way. In
relation to material space, for example, the case has been
made at length by Fogle (2011), but unfortunately he tends
to conceive physical space in terms of 'spatial syntax', which
is concerned with spatial configurations of accessibility – a
much narrower focus than time-geography, which deals with
the spatial distribution of experience much more generally.
Fogle also erroneously claims that phenomenology paid scant
attention to questions of space – the lifeworld and accompa-
nying notions of reach are *all about* space – and needlessly
suggests – since it adds nothing to analysis – that any capital
taking spatial form in some way should be called 'spatial
capital'. In relation to networks of interaction, furthermore,
the dialectic with fields has been raised somewhat sketch-
ily by Crossley (2013), who seems to be offering a more
reconciliatory position than other network theorists (e.g.
Becker, 2010: 372ff; see also de Nooy, 2003). Yet he tends to
focus only on the way in which webs of association with
fellow field protagonists shape one's position and strategy
within the field, making his account – ironically for someone

indebted to Merleau-Ponty – too exclusive phenomenologically. The 'conditionings' of a field or social space – the experiences sedimenting a desire for its forms of capital and instilling a sense of one's place and what is possible – can, after all, be delivered via direct interaction with people *outside* the field as well as through encounters with all manner of objects, spaces, symbols and signs produced and mediated by people at far spatio-temporal and social remove.

Relational phenomenology integrates and surpasses these insights to produce a fuller understanding of how the abstract relations of fields and social spaces shape and are shaped by the people, places, timings and objects of the lifeworld. So yes, on the one hand, fields structure the use and perception of space-time and the patterning of interaction in several ways. Absorbing the doxa of a field, and a sense of one's place in the distribution of capitals, overlays the perception of all things, stations, spaces, people, actions and timings with a particular meaning and pertinence, and the long-term and short-term strategies spurred by the struggle to attain capital generally entail specific movement of oneself through time-space, the setting into motion of chains of spatio-temporal travel for objects and other people, appropriation and naming of spaces and even the purposive forging of certain encounters, associations and networks. Two individuals physically co-present in the same 'situation' but not in the same field will, therefore, perceive one item, event, symbol, sign or person (including each other) presented to consciousness in two totally different ways and respond to them accordingly. A television interview is one thing to the journalist in the media field and quite another to the interviewed academic in the intellectual field, for example.

This is just one of the reasons why two individuals adjacent in a field may never have met or be particularly familiar with one another yet still produce similar works or have similar tastes and ideas. To give a concrete example, Crossley (2010) claims that the forces of social space cannot really explain the taste, in the UK, for football (soccer) amongst the dominated class and posits the necessity of social networks to fill the explicative hole, but with complete disregard for the historical development of football out of the 'street football' (or even 'kick the can') still played in poor neighbourhoods across the globe on account of it *being a disport requiring minimal equipment* (a ball or tin can plus maybe 'jumpers for goalposts') and rules to play, unlike the expensive equipment-filled sports of privileged youth such as tennis or rowing. It is, in other words, clearly attuned to specific conditions of existence associated with possession of certain capitals (see Holt, 1997; McKibbin, 1998), even if, admittedly, given *specificity* by idolization and emulation of local teams and players. Of course, its export into other national fields of sports with dissimilar structures of difference, such as in the United States, where it has been perceived as a feminine sport of the privileged opposed to American football, baseball and so on, is a different matter. Moreover, if or when people proximate in the same field meet for the first time, they are likely to feel an *affinity*, a *like-mindedness*, mediated by the perception of symbols and behaviours indicating their placement (cf. Lizardo, 2006). Conversely, two individuals far removed in the field may have regularly intersecting now lines, and even consider themselves friends of one sort or another, but their interaction will be premised on the mutual reading of their relative positionality via the associated signs – seeing one another as 'elitist' or 'populist', an 'upstart' or the 'old-guard', and so on.

At the same time, however, we have to acknowledge that interest in, entry into and awareness of the state of play of the field (including the specific meaning of objects, people and events) are nourished and modified through constant confrontation with things and successive interactions across time-space. Some of the latter will be mediated and unidirectional (e.g. textbooks, TV programmes, the internet) and some face-to-face. Sometimes they will be with people in the same field and sometimes with people not in the field (e.g. parents, teachers, journalists, etc.). Many will be routinized but some rarer, unique or novel – to different degrees depending on location and the density and range of a person's networks. And some will be actively sought but many will be imposed and simply 'there' by virtue of the interlaced time-space circuits of other people and objects. We also have to acknowledge that strategies are facilitated and limited by who or what can be mobilized when and where: those capability and coupling constraints mentioned earlier. The force of a field – its attraction and the sense of what can/is/must be done – is not some abstract pressure in the air pushing around isolated atoms, as Crossley (2010: 278) objects, but negotiated through active, situated engagement with all sorts of people and things, and that means those people and things, those specific encounters and material items, do make a difference to what one knows *of*, where one is/can be positioned *in* and how strongly one feels the pull *towards* the field. Heidegger, for example, would not have been who he was, and his philosophy would not have been what it is, had he not had the specific encounters (at conferences and in the classroom) and material spaces and objects (e.g. his famed hut, his books) he did through his life, even if the sediment left by these encounters, spaces and objects was filtered through the perceptual schemes accrued thereto.

There is one further nuance to add, however: the forces of different *kinds* of fields are mediated by networks in different ways. Bourdieu (1977, 1990b) himself, reflecting on his Algerian research in the light of studying France, drew a distinction between what he referred to as two 'modes of domination', or ways in which distributions of symbolic capital are maintained. On the one hand, there is, extending Mauss' (1954/2002) famous analysis, the 'elemental' form of domination characteristic of Kabyle communities whereby not just mutual orientation but differences of symbolic capital are maintained precisely through constant face-to-face exchanges – gifts, services, tribute, violence – between implicated players within a locality. We can put explicitly what Bourdieu only seemed to assume or hint at, however: this was still a field, with a topological structure, multiple implicated capitals (physical, economic, religious), an objective space of possible moves for each player, a habitus adjusted to that and strategies formulated accordingly, even if operating only at a local level (see Atkinson, 2015a). On the other hand, in contemporary, differentiated capitalist societies, institutionalized mechanisms (the state, the education system, the economy) maintain and regulate over time and space the legitimacy and value of capitals, or 'objectify' them, within the social space and fields without the need for constant direct person-to-person exchanges, meaning that field effects – knowledge of the state of play, shifts in capital and so on – are more likely to be mediated. The process through which that occurs, and the mechanism behind the historical transformation, we will return to shortly, but a point I want to emphasize, once again perhaps only making explicit what Bourdieu assumed, is that the *two modes of domination co-exist in contemporary societies*, with the structure and struggles of some fields being regulated by objectifying mechanisms while those of others – particularly the micro-fields of everyday life, including *local* social spaces and the family – continue to be more or less underpinned by regular, direct exchanges among a particular network of individuals.

Circuits of symbolic power

This leads us to the final advance our shift of perspective can offer: everyday practice, including entry into certain fields and the strategies that can be pursued in them, is conditioned by the cross-cutting movements of people, entities, symbols and signs generated by a multitude of struggles within myriad fields the agents of that practice are not themselves actually implicated in. Put another way, the position-takings generated by field forces ripple out from the relevant field members' worlds through specific overlapping time-space chains of objects, images and people, some regular and routinized, some infrequently or uniquely, and into the lifeworlds of others where they impact upon streams of experience and social surfaces not contending within the field. This includes the construction of particular cultural or technical artefacts, physical spaces and buildings, or the formulation of particular categories of thought and language, including which practices and movements in time-space are 'legal' or not (as in notions of 'trespass'). Obviously those possessing greater quantities of capital within their respective fields, being (mis)recognized 'authorities', wield disproportionate power to distribute their goods or definitions of reality in tune with their interests and to impose them as legitimate. Homologies *and* networks with players in the media, political, legal and bureaucratic fields, which possess widely recognized powers of consecration and distribution, facilitate that.[5] On the other hand, pathways into worlds are also conditioned to some degree by the capacities and propensities of 'consumers', and the receiving social surface, with its own history, will read the perceptual content through its existing typification schemes and in relation to its own combination of positions in social spaces and fields (as facilitating or impeding certain strategies, for example). This leads me to posit, in a similar fashion to Giddens (1984), a distinction between social structures on the one hand, which take the form of fields and social spaces, and a 'social order' on the other, with the latter comprising a distinct knot of intermeshing circuits of people and things in the global web carrying field effects over a specific band of time-space, sometimes received by people attuned to the game of origin and therefore spurring strategies or other position-takings, sometimes received by others not participating in that specific game but translating them into the logic of the fields they are invested in. Here, then, lies the missing principle of system integration.

The rudiments of such an idea do, to be fair, exist within Bourdieu's (1996b: 386; 1999a; 2000b: 102f; 2014) later writings in the form of 'legitimation circuits'. These are the chains of legitimating exchanges, the 'actions and reactions' between specific individuals, in which the symbolic content of a position-taking is recognized by those not within the field it was generated in. Historically tied up with efforts of state-building, these have, over time, become 'ever longer and more complex and thus more symbolically effective' (Bourdieu, 2000b: 103), giving rise to not only the differentiation of relatively autonomous fields in the field of power of a particular social order but to the institutional objectification of particular forms of capital mentioned earlier, that is to say, processes transforming them into symbolic capital amongst a wide population (cf. Bourdieu, 1990b). A prison guard's symbolic power within the micro-field of a prison, for example, is premised on a series of legitimating links between specific individuals up to the bureaucratic field and the legal field, while the legitimacy of certain qualifications as institutionalized cultural capital is guaranteed within a certain social order by a series of acts of recognition between players in the bureaucratic, legal and educational fields. Not much more is ever said on them, however, and like Elias' figurational sociology, from which the inspiration for the concept seems to have come, they seem to reduce spatio-temporal networks to a function of interdependence, thereby downplaying the differential distribution of knowledge and affordances they bring (Layder, 2006), and appear to be somewhat human-centric. We thus need to broaden their scope and recast them in terms of multiple, specific, intermeshing *circuits of symbolic power* through which the products and classifications generated in fields are continuously distributed over time-space through chains of association and movement and received not only by fellow field members but by the populace at large, shaping what people can think, do or say as well as when and where.

There are parallels with Marx (1956) on the circuits and metamorphosis of capital: any artefact or sign is distributed over time and space owing to the symbolic capital of the distributors in one or more fields and then implicated by receivers in one or more battles of their own for the same or different forms of symbolic capital. Yet the circuits of symbolic power are more encompassing, since what they distribute may not always be manifestly put to use in struggles for capital but simply form part of the background doxa. They move closer, in those instances, to the Foucauldian notion of capillary power, recognizing the dispersion of the effects of power throughout the whole social body and its function in shaping the 'possible field of action of others' (Foucault, 1982: 221), including through the 'government of things' (Lemke, 2015), but with three riders. First, as Wacquant (2009) points out, if the effects of power flow through capillaries, then we have to recognize the social order has a beating heart directing the current – the field of power. Second, the logic of homology dictates that the flow is a two-way, dialectical movement. Changes in tastes induced by changing conditions of existence will alter the specific position-takings of producers not only by supplying the orientations of newcomers to the field but by 'favouring the success, within the struggle constituting the field, of the producers best able to produce the needs corresponding to the new dispositions' (Bourdieu, 1984: 231) – all of which will be apparent to the producers not least through various time-space circuits of 'feedback' (social movements, focus groups, sales figures, etc.). Third, it is rarely a simple case of players in one field disseminating their definitions of reality in isolation; instead, there are complex relations of cross-field alliance and contestation, worked out through intermeshing circuits, which mediate and *co-produce* categories of thought and practices. Bourdieu (1993b, 1996a) himself acknowledged the significance of the interrelations between the field of artists, the field of critics and the field of galleries in the production of the perception of 'art' and the pure aesthetic within sections of the social space (which then, we might add, induces certain doxic rhythms in the family field, i.e. regular museum attendance – Bourdieu et al., 1991), though of course nowadays the role of the media field would have to be considered too.

So, any one material object or locale (as a configuration of objects) within one's world – a tin of beans, a book, a computer, a hut, a street – is the product of a collection of struggles within and between fields which has wended its way through specific chains weaving over time-space in disparate ways, directions and expanses from the producer(s), depending on their powers, and may then in turn be put to use in struggles within different fields. Take, for instance, a photocopier and its daily use in a company's office – an example picked out by Lahire (1998: 35) to demonstrate a mundane activity apparently inexplicable with Bourdieu's intellectual apparatus. What is this if not a category of object originally produced and subsequently tweaked in the conjoined struggles of scientific and economic fields and disseminated through specific time-space channels instituted by competitors of different standing within an economic field into specific physical sites, sometimes in a different nation, where bodies and perceptual schemes adjust to it and put it to routine and non-routine use in the pursuit of – and one might thus say it *makes possible* – firstly, the strategies of a firm within a *field of firms* within a sector of the same or another national economic field, as well as strategies within the *firm itself as a field* (cf. Bourdieu, 2000b: 203; 2005a)? Who is photocopying what and to what end, after all? An equally quotidian example, spotlighted by DeVault (1994: 65ff), might be the dialectical interplay between intended purchases in a routine grocery shopping trip, as a project flowing from a social surface attuned to (*inter alia*) class conditions and familial field relations, and the items actually available in the frequented stores thanks to the network of spatio-temporal distribution schedules enacted by firms across the globe. The same sort of logic extends to the imposition of rhythms of life – from 'clock time' and 'trading hours' (Thrift, 1981) through to school timetables and holiday periods (Bourdieu, 2014) – but more generally the various fields within national and international fields of power, as Bourdieu argued, operate to set and modify the relative conditions of existence of the populace – the very structure of national social space – by determining the availability and convertibility of capital through educational, fiscal and employment policy and practice.

Labels and classifications for all sorts of 'groups', 'movements' and 'types' of people and things in one field or another, or within the social/symbolic spaces, circulate thus too. Take, for instance, the category 'benefit claimant' – a more specific and mundane label than the notions of 'underclass' or 'feral youth' targeted by Wacquant (2009). Its definition and evaluation are struggled over in the different sections of the national field of power (religious, political, legal, intellectual, etc.) and filtered out directly or through intermediating fields from the individuals producing them in certain sites via such practices as teaching, social work, religious sermons, political speeches, legal rulings, newspaper columns, think tank research, official statistics and – as demonstrated in Dubois' (2010) incisive study of the circuits of symbolic power putting the players and products of the bureaucratic field directly in touch with its subjects – the humdrum interactions of those seeking welfare support with state agency workers sat at their kiosks. The teachers, social workers, journalists, television producers and state workers, as nodes in the circuits of symbolic power, come into contact with the orthodox and heterodox definitions put forward by dominant and dominated agents in the implicated fields – 'scroungers', 'a drain', 'the lazy' or 'the unfortunate', 'poor souls', 'the neglected' and so on, whether directly, via face-to-face interaction, or via documents, statements, circulars or the media. They then read them and the position-taking of the producer through the lens provided by their own social surface and corresponding interests and then, in turn, impart or apply their interpretation to others on the basis of their own symbolic power, including, in the case of the media field, through television programmes purporting to show what life on social welfare is 'really' like.

Bringing legitimation chains out of the shadows of Bourdieu's thought and remodelling them as circuits of symbolic power thus opens up a bounty of novel research avenues regarding the time-space distribution and reach of entities and categories of thought generated in fields and their importation into other spaces of contention, endowing, for example, many of the largest mutations sweeping social orders today with new intellectual pertinence. Just as Bourdieu drew inspiration from Elias' account of lengthening legitimation chains to posit the objectification of capital and the differentiation of national fields of struggle, so we can begin to explore the effects of more recent transport and communications technology generated within specific fields, especially the internet and social media, for the formation of, entry into, positions and strategies within, position-takings on and even exits from fields whose players may be at vast spatial remove from one another. How do YouTube, Facebook, Twitter and all the blogs, vlogs and such like – consummate annihilators of space through time, as Harvey (1989) might say – extend, challenge and reorient the customary circuits through which people are drawn towards, launch themselves into, are recognized or denigrated by others within and perceive the possible movements offered by any particular field, from the field of musical production or political practice to a familial cosmos and social spaces themselves? How are people from different locations on Earth differentially drawn into fields otherwise anchored to differing degrees in far-removed regions of the globe, and at what speeds and durations are their practices and participation 'turned over' compared to the past? How, therefore, are the bundles of circuits comprising social orders beginning to loosen, spill over and transcend traditional national borders? Such are some of the questions for twenty-first-century Bourdieusians, perhaps.

From mobility capital to motility

To finish, let me bring some of what has been argued so far to bear on the notion of 'mobility capital' mentioned near the start of the chapter, not just so as to expose the limits and needlessness of the concept, which is in any case confined to fairly specialist literature, but to extract from it a useful insight on spatio-temporal movement in a world where circuits of symbolic power and time-space paths increasingly cross borders in circumscribed ways. The idea has been pursued in a distinct strand of scholarship which, justifiably dissatisfied with the prevailing political concerns over 'access' privileging features of spaces rather than capacities of people, anchors it in the notion of 'motility' (Kaufmann, 2002; Kaufmann et al., 2004; Flamm and Kaufmann, 2006; see also Ohnmacht et al., 2009; Kaufmann, 2011). This term, extracted from biological science and recast in sociologized form, refers to the capacity of the individual to move over space through time, or the 'realm of possibilities for mobility' open to them (Flamm and Kaufmann, 2006: 168). It denotes *potential*; a latent ability underpinning the complex of projects people undertake in the world and manifesting in actual mobilities through time-space. Its constitution, say its advocates, is threefold. First, there is 'access', subtly reconceived as the individual's capacity to enter certain spaces at certain times taking into account not only economic costs but the spatio-temporal patterning of transport systems and destinations. Second, there is 'competence', or the individual's capacity to physically and cognitively master modes and systems of transport, from buses and bikes to cars and ferries. Finally, there is 'appropriation', which refers to the individual's desires, values and mental representations of modes of transport differentiating their likelihood of exploiting them. All of these phenomena, taken together under the umbrella of motility, are supposedly a new form of capital constitutive of class, claim Kaufmann et al. (2004), not only because they are irreducible to economic capital but because they are clearly convertible into other forms of capital, as people actualize their mobility potential to accrue economic, cultural or social capital.

The reasoning here, however, misinterprets the set of pertinent relations implicated in different mobilities and fudges cause and effect. 'Access' is determined largely by economic capital, evidently, but the residual element – the time-space patterning of transport and destinations in which the individual is situated – is too intricate to simply have the label of 'capital' slapped on it, not only because it is hardly a source of recognition or relative symbolic power in itself but because to do so is to fail to unpack its social constitution. As we have indicated, one's position in physical space in absolute terms and relative to others, the localization of things in space vis-à-vis people (schools, workplaces, shops, etc.) and the time-space organization of transport and communications infrastructure exist in complex dialectical relation with the struggles and strategies of class as well as other fields homologous with class. Demands for certain facilities (shops, schools, etc.) and willingness to travel to certain places will be conditioned in part by classed tastes and desires to accumulate economic and cultural capital, and these will, in turn, feed into the struggles within specific fields with power over the spatial supply of things and people (the state, businesses, local councils and so on). Via their circuits of symbolic power these then feed back into everyday classed conditions of existence and differentiate spatio-temporal affordances for the accumulation of economic, cultural and social capital and the development of specific tastes and perceptions. The neglect of the 'regions' in the United Kingdom at the expense of London by the players within the field of power, for example, as an outcome of specific strategies to maximize and concentrate capital, has made certain practices and strategies possible in one city yet not in another for people with similar capital stocks.

'Competence', moreover, denotes a basic practical mastery of transport types, which will patently depend on what has been available given classed resources, but it is hard to see how it acts as a specific capital separable from either access to vehicles (which depends on economic or social capital) or certification which can then return economic capital via labour (in which case it might be said to constitute a specific form of 'technical' capital; Bourdieu, 2005a). Finally, 'appropriation', of which the usual example is the affluent but eco-conscious cyclist, designates nothing other than classed dispositions and schemes of perception. Kaufmann et al. are content to see it as grounded simply in 'personal experience' and collective representations without rooting either within the social structures *differentiating* personal experience and power to impose one's representations as 'collectively' legitimate in the form of doxa (or at least orthodoxy). Ecological concern, for instance, as a political-attitude-cum-lifestyle betraying an ascetic disposition (refusal of excess, hedonism, etc.), corresponds closely with a particular section of the class structure – the rich in cultural capital, but less so economic capital (Eder, 1993; Atkinson, forthcoming b) – and returns *symbolic* capital insofar as it is construed, with more or less difficulty against the views of the less ecologically-minded economically rich, as the 'right' or 'good' thing to do more generally.[6]

Nevertheless, the analytical object that the notion of 'motility' is being used to construct – differentiated movement potential – is significant and, moreover, underexplored in the proliferating Bourdieusian research on the 'spatialization of class' (Savage, 2010: 115). Studies of gentrification, ghettoization, (s)elective belonging and such like, that is, as etchings into physical space and perceptions thereof of differences in social space, *assume* and *hint* at differences in motility – it is, indeed, the fundamental bedrock upon which the themes of interest are built – but never really dissect them in any detail. Still, to be useful motility has to be shorn of its extant theoretical baggage and reconceived not as a capital itself but as a complex *product* of capitals, class conditionings and circuits of symbolic power, thence generating differential possibilities for capital accumulation and dissemination of positon-takings.[7] It should be taken to designate, therefore, the range of objectively possible or necessary spatial movements given by the structures of the lifeworld, i.e. 'reach' in the sense given to that term by time-geographers, akin to the field of objectively possible movements in *social* space described by Bourdieu (1984: 110), and at the same time the *subjective* field of possibles this generates through the kinds of experience it yields, i.e. 'reach' in the sense given to that term by phenomenologists: a fuzzy and fallible sense of the feasible, doable and desirable which overlays perception of places and mobilities in particular contexts with an 'I can' or 'I want/need to' to different degrees (impossible, possible, probable, definite) as well as delimiting what is likely to enter consciousness in the first place. This operates, as Merleau-Ponty (2002) stressed, at a corporal level, in bodily protention and motor intentionality, but also in the formation of projects of varying magnitude to accrue or convert capital.

Of course, if our concern is field analysis, or class analysis, rather than analysis of individual lifeworlds, then we can locate principles of differentiation in frequencies, distances, destinations, durations and meanings of travel, that is, take the national and worldwide circuits of time-space paths and trace the *correspondences* with positions in social spaces (home *and* receiving) and their genesis in associated conditions and dispositions (necessity or distance therefrom, capital accumulation or distinction, etc.). One can, in so doing, distinguish layers of mobility and motility on the basis of temporality, beginning with the patterning of relatively routine travels through space furnishing a sense of a person's usual reach and 'territory', or lifeworld, moving through the infrequent and transitory pathways travelled for pleasure or work (e.g. 'business trips') to the longer-term displacements and relocations through the life course. If, however, our focus is lifeworld analysis, then we cannot content ourselves with class alone. The constitution of an empirical individual's motility, including migration (which can place individuals within two national social and symbolic spaces),[8] depends on, at one level, the specific state of national social spaces and their relations within a world system or global social space (cf. Sayad, 2004; Go, 2008) – with certain power-laden cultural or political relations, like those characterizing colonialism and its aftermath, facilitating or impeding possibilities. At another level, there is the individual's positioning within all kinds of other fields, big and small, and the *relations between them* in the lifeworld – i.e. their social surface, as integrated by the world horizon. The analytical task is to identify the web of factors implicated in the full shaping of protention and projection in the individual's lifeworld and unravel the relative place of locations within, and subjection to the effects of, separate spaces of struggle. Class will be a part of this, for sure, but so too will be, for example, the individual's employing organization – with its own relatively autonomous stakes, struggles and player strategies – and, in all probability, their family. Indeed, so central to most people's *Erlebnis* more generally is this last microcosm that we cannot hope to lay the groundwork for lifeworld analysis without subjecting it to focused sociological construction. To that task, then, we must now turn.

3

The Field of Family Relations

Among all the social forces competing for an individual's attention and devotion in their lifeworld, those of the family are paramount, not only because its stakes are ones over which almost everybody struggles but because they are often seen as the most important stakes of all. When people are asked what makes them happy, what 'comes first' and what they wish to protect at all costs, indeed what they would be most willing to die for, loved ones – partners, children, parents and others – are likely to top the list. Any attempt to try to map the social structures of everyday life and the experiences that shape the dispositions and desires of empirical individuals must, therefore, give it pride of place. Yet Bourdieu, for all his undoubted breadth of interest and influence and his vision of parent–child relations as the crucible of social reproduction, is hardly a leading figure in the sociology of the family. At best he is seen as offering some useful general pointers on the nature of practice, the rest of his substantive work then being left untouched on the assumption that it overemphasizes reproduction and treats the family as merely the conduit of capital transmission (Morgan, 1999: 21); at worst scholars of family life have savaged his oeuvre on the basis of – to turn Silva's (2005: 89) assessment of Bourdieu's engagement with feminist theory on her own enquiry – a 'narrow and flimsy grasp' of it. He is thus unfairly pilloried for universalizing the nuclear model, unjustly challenged for prioritizing the role of the father, wrongly chastised for his ignorance of internal family struggles, and misguidedly dismissed with such force that subsequent keystone texts decline to even bother with him (e.g. Smart, 2007: 193).

The exceptions to this trend are those studies with a particular interest in the relationship between family and class, but the conceptualization of the former concept in these cases is so weak as to work against any chance of someone flying the Bourdieusian flag, even if loosely, being taken seriously by mainstream analysts of the family. In the US, for example, Annette Lareau's (2000, 2003) high-profile Bourdieu-influenced work on 'class, race and family life' has lucidly laid bare the stark contrasts in pace of life, adult–child relations and pedagogy between the classes, but stayed rather more reticent on precisely what 'family' is taken to be in all this. The best we get is a rather brief and superficial description of it, in thoroughly non-Bourdieusian terms, in the language of norms and institutions (Lareau, 2003: 14–15), plus a useful but desperately undertheorized distinction between 'actualized' and 'unactualized' resources (2003: 277–8). It remains unclear, as a result, whether and how family relations have their own relatively autonomous influence on practice or whether, as seems to be the case in the empirical analysis, they are treated as essentially the scene in which class and race are simply acted out (the same could be said for Devine, 2004). In the UK, on the other hand, Gillies' (2007) study of 'working-class motherhood' works with a Bourdieusian understanding of class but then, when it comes to family, relies on the limited conceptualization provided by the Foucault-inspired, while Reay et al. (2005) problematically extend the concept of habitus to the family level to understand shared attitudes and practices, obscuring thereby the internal hierarchies and struggles that sociologists of the family have been investigating for decades (Atkinson, 2011a).

This is a rather sorry state of affairs, but also an entirely unnecessary one. For Bourdieu does, in fact, offer a robust means of conceptualizing 'family life'; a means which not only incorporates the advances of contemporary scholarship on the family but surmounts its limits, thus furnishing a comprehensive grasp of the particularities of this social phenomenon, its place among larger power structures and its pivotal role in the specification, complication and even derailment of social and cultural reproduction. This is the notion of the family as a relatively autonomous *field* with its own doxa, its own struggles and its own forms of domination. Such a conceptualization is present, though admittedly underemphasized, in Bourdieu's earlier work on matrimonial strategies and kinship amongst the Berbers of Kabylia and the peasants of Béarn. Here, against anthropology's taste for genealogical taxonomies and structuralist notions of rules, he envisioned the family in terms of 'practical kinship', defining it as 'the field of relationships that are constantly re-used' and reinforced in everyday practice and exchange with its 'community of dispositions and interests', 'self-representations' and efforts to maintain itself as a united and solidary 'group', including with a specific constructed past which dominant agents within it profess, but also its internal 'power relations', 'conflict of interest', 'tensions' and struggles over membership and boundaries (see especially Bourdieu, 1990b: 162–99; 1990c: 59–75). But it was in 1993, in a short paper for *Actes de la Recherche en Sciences Sociales*, seemingly written off the back of *La Misère du Monde*, a book teeming with familial tensions and conflicts, that he first explicitly, albeit briefly, tendered the notion that the 'family' functions as a field like any other (reprinted in Bourdieu, 1998). Some further flesh was added to these bare bones in somewhat elliptical and fleeting, yet potentially very important, meditations a few years later (Bourdieu, 2000b: 164ff), but after that there was nothing more, not even in his own self-socioanalysis (Bourdieu, 2007).

Some Bourdieusian scholars, it is true, resist the idea that the family constitutes a field, despite Bourdieu's own statements to this effect, on the basis of a rather narrow definition of field relations (see e.g. Benson and Neveu, 2005: 20n14), but others, without delving into the necessary conceptual clarification and elaboration, have begun to realize that this concept might just be critical for making sense of both gender relations and childhood (McNay, 1999; Alanen, 2011; Alanen et al., 2015). In fact, though these are indeed areas of particularly acute salience, because the family is so fundamental to structuring everyday lifeworlds and social surfaces its import is even wider than that. Ironically, then, in order to fully lay the foundations for lifeworld analysis, open up new possibilities for research under the banner of relational phenomenology and set the stage for the analysis of social becoming and gender in the following chapters, there is a need to train our sights on the structure and dynamic of a particular (type of) field. Using Bourdieu's own brief reflections as a springboard and drawing on extant research, therefore, this chapter explores and develops the constitutive elements of family *qua* field – its specific *doxa*, the internal struggles over *capital*, its *boundaries* and its embeddedness in a wider *universe* of familial relations. To begin with, however, the *genesis* of familial fields in the quotidian realization of the common yet contested category of thought that is 'family' will be traced.

'Family' as contested category

'Family', 'household', 'kinship', 'home' and so on are labels possessing no foundational essence or universal substance – not consanguinity, genetic lineage, conjugal roles and functions or even, as espoused by some recent Elias-influenced researchers (Connolly, 2004; Widmer, 2010; Lahire, 2011), specific relations of interdependency. This we know from the sheer variety of patterns of living and linguistic distinctions used across and within cultures and epochs (see Burguière et al., 1996), and, indeed, from the shifting content of the very signifier 'family' in earlier centuries (Williams, 1983: 131–4). It is, instead, a set of common perceptual schemes or typification bundles, that is, a classificatory system in which 'family' is treated *as if* it had a timeless essence and natural basis, an existence *sui generis* and palpable purpose, with which agents carve up the social universe and organize experience. However, while this principle of perception may be so widespread as to constitute 'common sense', or doxa as Bourdieu would say, by no means is its precise sense commonly constituted. It is and has long been, instead, a stake in the struggles between the various protagonists in a pertinent – local, national, international – *field of power*. Composed of agents from the dominant class and, contrary to any crude class reductionism, the dominant gender to different degrees by field, they tend to represent the dominant interest and, as such, impose the definition of reality favourable to the perpetuation of the advantages possessed by the dominant. Yet, being composed of constitutive fields in which different capitals are accorded different values (the economic field, political field, field of cultural production, etc.), there are also different *versions* of the dominant interest within the field of power and thus struggles to impose different versions of the dominant vision of reality. There are, in fact, dominant and dominated sections of the field of power and, therefore, an *orthodox* definition of reality contending against *heterodox* ones (Bourdieu, 1977), differentially dispersed to the populace through the circuits of symbolic power leading out from the agents and sub-fields of the field of power: practices of teaching, midwifery or social work, religious speeches, political statements, legal rulings, newspaper stories, official statistics and so on (cf. Bourdieu, 1998: 71–3).

In the case of 'family', 'household', etc., the current orthodoxy in the Western world, shaped by literally millennia of struggles and strategies amongst dominant agents (see Lenoir, 2003) yet falsely universalized by early forms of psychoanalysis and its functionalist appropriators (e.g. Parsons and Bales, 1956), has undoubtedly been a consanguineous, heterosexual, patriarchal, monogamous, private, nuclear, male breadwinner/female homemaker model.[1] One need only look to national laws and practices on maternity and paternity leave, the assumptions of much developmental psychology or even the United Nation's decree, enshrined in article 16 (3) of the Universal Declaration of Human Rights, that the family is 'the natural and fundamental unit' to see this. Yet there are two identifiable levels of contention today. On the one hand, there is the struggle between the different versions of consanguineous, heterosexual, etc., family espoused by the fraction of the field of power richer in *cultural* capital – intellectuals (including Giddens, 1992, 1998), therapists, educators, etc. – and the version propagated via a league of think tanks by the section of the field of power richer in *economic* capital. If the former vaunt democratic decision making and childrearing, reflexivity and disclosure, diversity and change, cultural enrichment of children and heavy (maternal) involvement or 'support' in their education, then the latter favour traditional gendered divisions of labour, paternal authority, firm marriage and strictly limited interference by the state. Seeping in different combinations into the family policy of successive governments depending on the precise balance of power and homologies in the field of power, in both cases, as Edwards (2010) and others have pointed out, practices of the dominated class are accordingly pathologized as either outdated and unsupportive or morally devoid and economically draining (Walkerdine and Lucey, 1989; Lawler, 2000; Gillies, 2007). On the other hand, allied to the cultural fraction and counterposed to the conservative version of the orthodoxy has been a growing *radical heterodoxy* in which non-blood, non-heterosexual and non-nuclear definitions, as well as family constructions stemming from minority ethnic and religious creeds, have become more a part of contemporary experience and given a level of formal recognition (Bourdieu, 2001: 88ff; Weeks, 2007). Nevertheless fierce struggles continue, if not in law then in the media, political and religious fields and in everyday parlance, over whether or not these constitute 'real' families, with the heterosexual nuclear model remaining dominant in Western nations and generating all manner of acts of symbolic and physical violence (Weeks, 1991; Goldberg-Hiller, 2004). Furthermore, it is noticeable that even within this 'war over the family', as Berger and Berger (1983) would describe it, the heterodoxies and orthodoxies still share many utterly doxic yet thoroughly historical assumptions – romantic love, cohabitation and privatism chief amongst them (though see Roseneil, 2006).

The category realized

If 'family' is a circulating category of perception, however, it is, according to Bourdieu, a *realized* one. In other words, people are thrown into a world in which this category, and its associated vocabulary, is simply there from the start, that is, infused in all the injunctions and sayings framing the expectations and practices of everyday life which, pregnant with unarticulated assumptions, implicit definitions and pedagogy, 'construct an affective object and socialize the libido' (Bourdieu, 1998: 68): from 'say dada' and 'mommy loves you' to 'when you get married . . .', 'when you have kids . . .', 'be nice to your sister', 'that's what mothers are for' and 'blood is thicker than water'. This process will be unpacked in greater detail in the next chapter; for now we can note that through appropriation of the attendant lexis – generally delivering the dominant definitions of reality, but in some instances shaped by the heterodox definitions of family imbued in more ambiguous and unsure injunctions ('*if* you get married . . .', 'if that's your thing . . .', 'you don't have to . . .') – children develop complexes of semantic and emotional associations, pairings and recipes of action and thus become disposed to recognize certain others as 'kin' of various designations, to feel towards them in certain ways (loyalty, care, obligation, affection, love, or anxiety, guilt, etc., if not), do certain things for them (physical mainte- nance, educational support, etc. – see Finch, 1989; Finch and Mason, 1993) and to close ranks. Fostering routine sharing and the sharing of routine, this, in turn, consolidates care and integration, with two ultimate consequences: first, it gives apparent legitimacy to the notion that the world is divided into these things called 'families' (Bourdieu, 1998: 67–8); and second, it provides the generative principle of all the varying strategies, adapted to pooled capital possession, aimed at securing symbolic recognition for offspring (wanting 'the best' for them, for them to 'do well') and, insofar as they act as representatives of the perceived collective, for 'the family' too (Bourdieu, 1994, 1998: 69–70).

People are not, however, simply drilled, regulated or 'produced' through the orthodox and heterodox principles of (di)vision flowing through the circuits of symbolic power, as the Foucault-inspired would have it (e.g. Donzelot, 1980; Rose, 1999). Instead, people read them through the schemes of perception constructed in the course of experience in their socially structured lifeworlds, harness them to their own conditions of existence and practices across fields and – via their homologues or spokespeople in the field of power – can challenge and reshape orthodoxy and heterodoxy. Hence the steady consolidation of the private, nuclear and sentimental family as the dominant model in Western societies from the eighteenth to the twentieth centuries was associated with not only the shifting struggles in differentiating fields of power, specifically the declining authority of the religious field and the rise of a new dominant class with both economic and – contrary to Engels' (1986) reductive thesis – cultural fractions concerned to safeguard their respective new-found patrimonies (see Lenoir, 2003; Bourdieu, 2004b). Also important were, *inter alia*, falling infant mortality rates providing the conditions for greater investment and interest in children, the decline of service hewing servants from the perception of 'family', and the switch from local matrimonial strategies oriented towards family interest to elective affinity and romantic love as the general principle of conjugation following the unification of the marriage market brought by the development of national economic fields, urbanization and mobility (Bourdieu, 2008: 165ff; cf. Shorter, 1976; Ariès, 1996). Similarly, in the more recent past, the increase in female economic independence with the growth of highly gendered welfare state employment and women's educational opportunities in Western nations, coupled with pressures from sexually liberal elements of the intellectual field and the advance of the romantic conception of marriage, engendered a shift in political and legal constructions of divorce which, in turn, accelerated divorce rates, remarriage rates, step-family formation, single parenthood and so on, begetting in part the current orthodoxies and heterodoxies described above (see Phillips, 1991).

Not all appropriations and reinterpretations, however, are equally likely to gain recognition. The dominant definition of 'good mothering', for instance, tends to represent the practices of the dominant ethnicity and the dominant class, or at least the cultural fraction thereof, possible only with the possession of certain resources. In many instances, therefore, it produces shame and guilt amongst those who, with less symbolic capital within the ethno-national space (Hage, 1998) and/or economic and cultural capital and drawing on local, practical models and methods of coping rather than the latest 'official' advice, are unable to provide the forms of interaction, pedagogy and support demanded. Yet, in the determined bid to see themselves as 'good mothers', some still endeavour to cohere their own practices with reinterpreted elements of this definition (e.g. claiming to be giving their children 'healthy' food by avoiding fast food), even if ultimately discredited by the representatives of symbolic power (Perrier, 2010), or even steadfastly resist and criticize it in a bid to assert their own orientations as valuable, albeit without the symbolic capital to impose their own orientations as even a heterodoxy (cf. Atkinson, 2010a: 168–71).

The family-specific doxa

One corollary of the disjuncture between definitions filtering out from the field of power and practice is that, alongside the society-wide perceptions of what does or should constitute 'family' in general, as visible in political speeches and television programmes as on the back of cereal boxes (cf. Goffman, 1976), is a perception of what constitutes '*my* family' or '*this* family' – i.e. the *family-specific* doxa. The latter is, to be precise, the taken-for-granted, unquestioned and shared (intersubjective) sense of 'what is done' or 'to be done' in 'this family', distinct from other families, manifest and sustained in all the elements of ordinary life which, like Plato's decree inscribed above the Academy of Athens to 'let no-one ignorant of geometry enter here', act as barriers to entry for outsiders. It is rooted in the nature of shared experience produced by the generic patterns of living that form the embodiment and enactment of the current generalized family doxa, principally the assumption that 'families' or intimates will share a living space, closed off from the 'public sphere' or 'community' (Allan and Crow, 1989), but also, more generally, that mothers, fathers, etc., act in certain ways towards one another. Indeed the latter cluster of assumptions act to bolster family-specific doxa when co-presence is, for one reason or another, not so frequent, since it disposes each to attend to what others are doing, to different degrees, through regular updates (just as one artist might keep track of another's work in the artistic field). The construction of the 'family' or its uniting doxa are not, therefore, coterminous with the 'household', another (related but separable) perceptual category – they usually extend far beyond it in time and space, while cohabitees need not be united by specifically familial constructions (cf. Allan and Crow, 2001). Yet since the generalized assumptions revolving around family life are given particular form by the capitals possessed in different fields by each member, their circulation between family members and gendered dispositions and expectations, so too is the family-specific doxa. Thus, for example, we can give flesh to Bourdieu's (1990b: 54; also Bourdieu and Passeron, 1979: 12) sketchy remarks that 'forms of the division of labour between the sexes', 'household objects', 'modes of consumption', 'parent–child relations', 'domestic morality' and so on comprise the 'familial manifestations of necessity'.

Elements of the family-specific doxa, binding the agents into a perceptual 'we' ('*we* do this', 'what *we* like'), include, first of all, the taken-for-granted interweaving of time-space paths, routines, rhythms and regionalizations (Giddens, 1984; Morgan, 2011): timing and nature of mealtimes and housework, specific chairs or places for specific family members ('dad's chair'), the hub of the house ('the place to be'), bathroom sequences, timing of visits, telephone calls or emails, who lives where and so on. Then there is family-specific language, that is, the formulation of specific 'nick-names', phrases and words associated with people – whether within the field or beyond it, like those seen regularly during the routine round of time-space paths – or places – a house, a room, a holiday retreat and so on. Either overlaying an existing word or phrase with a fresh significance or conjuring neologisms, in both cases forged through shared experiences then carried forward in them, they remain semantically impenetrable to the outsider. Family-specific stories, myths, maxims, mottoes and, allied to them, specific objects (including heirlooms and photographs) acting as symbols of shared experience and belonging are related to this (see Gillis, 1996; Smart, 2007).

The ultimate bedrock of family-specific doxa, however, is what Berger and Luckmann (1991: 74) called 'reciprocity of typification'. Each person disposed to envision themselves as part of 'this family' and recognized as such synthesizes the repeated experience of the deeds and the words of the others perceived to comprise it – pairing, associating, typifying, categorizing – such that, on perceiving or attending to them and their flow of conduct in any slice of time, there is, in the horizon of consciousness, an anticipation of what is likely to come next, of what they are likely to do or say, or, in short, of what is possible and impossible, probable and improbable, usual and unusual ('I know you', 'I know what you're like'). This does not presuppose any form of 'disclosing intimacy' (Giddens, 1992; Jamieson, 1998), nor even, as Berger and Kellner (1964) seemed to assume, plenty of conversation – both notions bearing the classed vision of those hypothesizing them (Wiley, 1985; Edwards, 2010). Typification and classification occur pre-predicatively simply in the course of repeated experience of one another.

As with any element of doxa – and as evidenced by the stupefaction, rationalization or dismissal reported by Garfinkel's (1984: 47–8) intrepid students when directed to breach it – it is perhaps most observable when confounded, calling forth verbalized disbelief ('that's not like you'). Yet the appresentation of the other's stock of knowledge and framing dispositions, feeding into protention and calling forth responses, is generally confirmed in everyday practice and woven seamlessly into co-constructed and co-realized projects. One need only look, for example, to all those ubiquitous, almost imperceptible – if not halted by all those little phrases that populate routine interaction ('I know what you're going to say', 'here we go', 'I knew that was coming') – instances in which members of familial fields finish each other's sentences and co-construct narratives. It may be premised on familiarity with the other's dispositions, or compounded by a harmony of dispositions and reference to co-experienced events, but as the words of the other course through the stream of consciousness they are attended at all times by an anticipation of what is likely to come next, given what they know of them and the flow of the discourse (perhaps the story has even been told before), to the extent that each almost 'thinks with' the other, prompting, directing and completing statements together.

There are several facets of reciprocal typification which, despite being so enmeshed, can be unpicked. First, perception of the other in any instance inherently involves appresentation of their accumulated knowledge of both oneself and the other members of the family – evident in all those instances when we are inclined to say 'you know me' or 'you know what (s)he's like'. Second, typification and categorization of the tastes of significant others colours not only the perception of the people in question, but the perception of items, places, practices and ideas too. That is to say, certain perceptual inputs are apperceived through schemes of interpretation articulating not only one's own tastes ('I like that') but the perceived tastes of others as well, whether as an imposed relevance (e.g. selecting a birthday gift, choosing a school) or in those moments where an item suddenly lifts out of the background, like a Gestalt, and presents itself as something '(s)he would like' – '(s)he'd go for that', 'that's him/her' – or the inverse ('I can't see him/her liking that', 'it's not your thing').

Third, as Merleau-Ponty stressed, reciprocal typification and protention are often *corporeal*, encompassing the reading of the comportment of the other and the unfurling of motor actions in reply. A particular expression, gesture or posture can be saturated with accumulated significance and expectation ('don't give me that look', 'I know your game', etc.), and is particularly pronounced in instances where language skills are still developing among younger children and parents must infer more from bodily conduct. It is also especially clear in instances where family members play sports or games together in which particular techniques and tactics – sporting and familial at one and the same time – have become routinized ('dad always does that', 'that's his favourite trick') or, especially with younger children, playfully wrestle, dance, cuddle, etc., together, with each move (a swing of an arm, readying to jump, etc.) pre-predicatively, through motor intentionality, adjusted to the perceived capacities and motility of the other(s), which may mildly misfire ('you're getting heavy'), as well as emerging tendencies (nipping, pinching, getting more boisterous, etc.). And then of course there is perception of the other's *sexual* dispositions (what 'turns them on').

Fourth, typification and categorization of others involves the interpenetration of multiple *levels of generalization*. Just as Schutz's (1970: 56–7) dog was intuited not only as an Irish setter, with species-typified characteristics, but as *his particular* Irish setter, Fido, with his idiosyncratic behaviours, in other words, so too players in the family field are perceived as personifications of general types and – because of the frequent experience distinguishing them from strangers

– as unique 'personalities', with descriptions and judgements seamlessly oscillating between and blending levels in the course of everyday practice dependent upon the task at hand. To brand another as a typical example of a general type is, in such cases, to accuse – and as Bourdieu liked to point out, the word 'categorize' is derived from the Greek *kategoria*, to accuse publically – and it is only through such banal applications and judgements (which also include tropes of 'girls are like that', 'boys will be boys', 'well he is a boy' and such like) that systems of symbolic difference are sustained and reproduced. It is, indeed, especially significant when parents describe children in seemingly innocuous mid-level categories that represent, even if only loosely, vaguely or subtly, open to interpretation or *allodoxia*, practices and modes of being corresponding with certain sectors of social space – 'a reader', 'a doing child', 'a practical kind of guy', 'creative', etc. – because they can, in many ways, act as *self-fulfilling prophecies* insofar as the other so-labelled not only is treated as such but integrates the designation into their self-conception, projection, libidinal charge and dispositions (cf. Laing, 1971: 78ff).

Fifth, a facet of reciprocal categorizations and typifications – and indeed of typification in general – underemphasized by mainstream phenomenology is the fact that they are intrinsically *relational*, inherently involving implicit and explicit comparison against what the percept is *not* within a system of difference. This may relate to a multitude of spaces of difference, but within the family it is often overlaid by contrasts, comparisons and perceptual coalitions (or 'groups') of implicated family members under various descriptions, mobilizing the multiple levels of generality already seen, from the point of view of one's own position. Although usually unstated and fuzzy, only occasionally surfacing in conversation, when put in a situation in which they are prompted to talk about their family (with teachers, family friends, inquiring sociologists, etc.) they flow forth easily enough. It could be parents distinguishing sociable versus independent children, 'creative' and 'arty' daughters versus 'sciency' sons, or generally describing children as 'just like me' or 'like their (grand)mother/(grand)father/auntie/cousin, etc.', or whether it is siblings defining themselves against each other in relation to one or other property securing some form of recognition in the eyes of parents, teachers and so on (as being 'smarter' or 'better at sports', etc.) (Davies, 2015).

A product of all of the above, finally, is subjective anticipation of the likely longer-term future of each member of the family and, with them, of the family as a whole. When encoded in everyday speech – whether as an assumption of educational destiny, as well as likely subjects and professions ('when you're at university . . .', 'you could be a . . .'), or an awareness of limits ('that's not for the likes of us', ' she's not likely to . . .') – these act as 'calls to order', sustaining the field of possible actions in the double sense of *probability*, the tacit anticipation of the likely fates inscribed in conditions of life given by gender, ethnicity and position in the social space and of what is *'right'*, in line with the moral dispositions, or the ethos, making a virtue of necessity.

Family as field of struggle

So, whilst there may be a set of shared assumptions and orientations uniting a certain constellation of agents, the notion of family-specific doxa breaks with purely phenomenological or ethnomethodological approaches, including their current 'family practices' incarnation popular in the UK (e.g. Morgan, 1996, 2011), insofar as it recognizes the embeddedness of those assumptions in wider structures of power and privilege. There is, however, a second rupture too, for insofar as those agents cohered by a family-specific doxa possess different levels of authority to set and enforce its elements (i.e. symbolic capital) yet engage in struggle over them, they become part of a system of objective structural relations, that is to say, a *field* (Bourdieu, 1998: 68–70). Differences over what should be done and what is right – whether in terms of the future trajectories of offspring, the household division of labour, political proclivities, sexuality, elements of lifestyle (music, clothing, etc.), or all the small regionalizations ('that's my chair!'), routines ('why do you always have to do that?'), typifications ('you don't know me at all!') and so on – thus, as in any other field, splinter the doxa into a conservative *orthodoxy* and subversive *heterodoxy* to greater and lesser degrees, with different alliances, factions, rifts and, ultimately, levels of recognition. Though these struggles and stances are by no means reducible to the household level, implicating non-residents in their contestation, the organization of agents into shared dwellings thanks to the internalization of dominant definitions of familial or intimate life, not least via state policies (tax, inheritance, welfare) which presuppose and encourage them (cf. Bourdieu, 1998: 65, 71–2; 2005a: 12, 20–1), does have the particular effect of fracturing the field into so many constitutive 'domestic (sub)spaces', as Bourdieu (2000b) called them, with their own orientations towards the overriding doxa and intense struggles mediating and mediated by the structure of the wider familial field.

The specific symbolic power, or capital, of the field, i.e. the capacity to be taken seriously in determining what is and should be done within the family, derives from a number of sources, some of them somewhat heteronomous (economic capital, physical capital, etc.), but one of them – a particularly important one – being peculiar to the family: *love*. In other words, love – or affective recognition, being cared about, depended upon and so on – is not just a straightforward and evenly distributed product of the practical realization of 'family', but *functions as a relatively autonomous form of capital with currency in this particular cluster of relations*. Evidently it is unlike the capitals that operate in many other fields in contemporary societies insofar as it bears a very low degree of objectification, i.e. institutional validation and regulation. The mode of domination within familial fields is thus more akin to that of the localized social spaces in which symbolic capital was judged, mystified and struggled over in pre-capitalist society, or those still existing in some locales today, i.e. maintained via constant interpersonal exchanges (including through gift giving, favours, displays of interest/care, or disinterest, direct threats and violence), but that makes its structure no less topological. Moreover, to view love and care as a capital is not to reduce it to economistic or instrumentalist principles, as some might fear, but merely an acknowledgement of the fundamental datum that to love and be loved is at once one of the earliest and most pervasive of human desires and one of the most basic yet arbitrary forms of power over others. Bourdieu (2001: 109–12), it is true, suggested 'pure love' may represent a suspension of relations of domination, but love is no different from any other principle of recognition *qua* capital: relative possession grants utter fulfilment and contentment while also always being a symbolic power *in potentia* via the submission of others ('I'd do anything for you') and the explicit or perceived (in this case through anger, disappointment, etc.) threat of diminishment – with the lack of this capital, experienced as a sense of being unloved, uncared for, not taken seriously and so on, being one of the most wretched forms of symbolic denigration there is.[2]

Digression: From 'emotional capital' to love as capital

In an earlier iteration of this argument I suggested that love might be referred to as 'emotional capital', twisting an existing concept theorized by, among others, Nowotny (1981), Allatt (1993), Illouz (1997), Gillies (2006) and, perhaps most influentially, Reay (2000, 2004). Subsequent reflection has made it clear, however, that while the users of that term do tap into something important, the concept is so problematic that it is best to not simply avoid it but explicitly dispense with it in an exercise of clearing away errors all the better to sharpen our own constructs. Purporting to grasp the emotional 'investments' made by parents – particularly mothers – in enhancing or buffering their child's journey through the twenty-first-century education system, the core argument of Reay and the others would seem to be that, alongside the normal Bourdieusian triad of economic, cultural and social capital, a particular emotional style serves as another resource that can be passed from parent (specifically mother) to child via involvement in the latter's schooling to ensure educational success – it too therefore generates a 'profit' insofar as it is converted into cultural capital. In practice, it appears to cover communication of emotions in relation to education; sensitive, sympathetic encouragement and support of schoolwork (Reay, 2000: 582); and confidence and enthusiasm over one's child's progression – all visible in patient or prickly assistance with homework and discussions of behaviour. Reay (2000) is, however, troubled by the fact that while investment of emotional capital can generate positive outcomes (establishing high expectations and the importance of education) it can produce negative ones too (resistance and anxiety amongst children). Consequently, though 'middle-class' mothers are generally held to possess more emotional capital than their working-class peers because they are more 'emotionally involved' in their child's schooling, it does not correspond straightforwardly with educational success. Such a 'complex contradiction' (Reay, 2000: 583), she prudently concedes, means more theoretical puzzle-solving is needed. Moreover, Gillies (2006), worried that Reay's usage entwines emotional capital too closely to educational success and thus dominant mores, urges a broadening of the term to cover the emotional 'investments' made by *all* parents in support of their children's *general* well-being, including generating self-esteem, worrying over and trying to secure future prospects and fighting back against perceived injustice or victimization at school. Even so, she laments, the notion remains 'conceptually slippery', difficult to delimit and, to her mind, awkwardly encased in an economistic metaphor potentially 'rationalizing' emotions (Gillies, 2006: 292).

Ultimately, however, the glitches identified by Reay and Gillies are symptoms of the concept's deeper flaws. For one thing, despite capital being an inherently *relational* notion, it is not especially clear within which set of structural relations this particular resource is supposed to derive its meaning (Grenfell, 2010: 25). If, like Reay, we follow Illouz (1997) and see emotional capital as simply a specific form of cultural capital, the implication is that it mingles in the social space of classes along with economic, generic cultural and social capital – a move which not only underpins Reay's and Gillies' reservations, but offers a reductive account of the genesis and meaning of familial affect. One simply cannot make sense of the warmth, pleasure, frustration, prickliness, disappointment, etc., of familial relations vis-à-vis education, or anything else, without factoring in the emotional history and power balance between mother and child and the embeddedness of this particular relation within the structure of authority and affection characterizing the broader family, all of which emotional capital ignores. On the other hand, if, like Gillies, we break from Illouz's work and generalize emotional capital to *all* families without further conceptual specification, then not only does it float free from any structural context but ceases to function as a *principle of (mis)recognition*, i.e. a reason for being functioning at the same time as a form of perceived legitimacy or power, over which sets of agents *struggle* – the bedrock definition of capital established in Bourdieu's (2000b) philosophical work. Better, then, to forget about trying to label emotional 'investment' in education as a capital on the basis of false economic analogy and instead focus on how struggles for love within familial fields – especially domestic sub-fields – entwine with the classed and gendered desires, expectations and hopes of parents for their children, with all the emotional fallout that brings when aspirations go unfulfilled.

The distribution of powers

Love is, however, only one principle of power within the familial field and, moreover, is itself entwined with other principles of domination – the family field is, after all, only a *relatively* autonomous system of struggle, to different degrees in different instances. Masculine domination – i.e. the monopolization of certain capitals, particularly physical and economic capital (including in the form of property rights), sometimes codified in law – is, and has long been, paramount here, though to an (unevenly) declining extent across the globe (Therborn, 2004). Domestic violence is the most patent expression, but it manifests more routinely in such practices as women cooking what the man wants to eat (DeVault, 1994), carrying out the majority of the housework even when in paid employment (Hochschild, 1989), or deferring to and orienting childrearing towards the male's directives on their offspring's educational and occupational future ('your father knows best'). Yet it is not necessarily always so straightforward. Where women possess greater economic, cultural or other capital (e.g. sexual) relative to others and/or relative to their partner – with the greater representation of women in higher education and their greater economic independence due to feminization of the workforce providing particular historical context here – there may be greater parity or contestation.[3] They may even act as 'the boss', the dominant force in the family enforcing 'what is done' on educational matters or consumption practices, with more or less struggle from the male (cf. Oakley, 1976; McRae, 1986; Pahl, 1989; Kaufmann, 2009), though one must not confuse simply 'making the decisions' or running the family finances with symbolic power as the former may still be directed towards satisfying the tacit demands and expectations of others within the field at one's expense (Allan and Crow, 2001). Gender should not be considered merely a division between parents either, but something which can pit siblings against one another (visible in scuffles, name-calling and put-downs), or which can be the basis of specific parent–child coalitions – not necessarily because of shared gender but due to shared perceptions of 'proper' gendered behaviour.

This brings us, secondly, to age, or, more accurately, generation. There is, of course, a direct parallel here with Bourdieu's writings on other fields, especially the fields of cultural production, where newer (generally younger) generations of players (artists, writers, etc.), initially entering the field with somewhat less capital, appear more likely to take up heterodox and subversive positions, successfully or unsuccessfully challenging the conservative orthodoxy of the capital-rich older generations. Thus one could conjecture that, at least in societies like many of those in the West where elders have lost the veneration once accorded to them, advancing age – and all that can come with it (children setting up their own households, post-retirement diminution of economic capital, etc.) – tends to bring a certain loss of power within the family field relative to younger generations, rendering the once dominant, the upholders of orthodoxy, the declining conservative rear-guard of the field. When it comes to younger children and their parents in the household, however, the parallel becomes much more complicated. This particular element of struggle is, today, hinged upon constructions of 'childhood' and 'parenthood', fed especially by the field of developmental psychology, emphasizing specific characteristics and capacities (vulnerability, emotional needs, dependency, *doli incapax*, ages of 'consent', of 'maturity', etc.) and thus manufacturing and sanctioning, through their internalization as schemes of perception, certain relations of subordination and authority (Alanen and Mayall, 2001; Gillies, 2007; Burman, 2008).

Yet the child is no passive recipient of inculcation. As emphasized by childhood scholars for decades (e.g. James and Prout, 1990, 1996; Smart et al., 2001; James, 2013), notwithstanding the voluntarist assumptions that sometimes go with it, and contrary to what is usually assumed about Bourdieu's model of the social world, the child can – depending on field and wider social conditions – be an active participant and challenger in the game, repelling and attempting (with varying levels of success) to subvert the parental orthodoxy in the struggle for recognition. This is not reducible merely to 'adolescent rebellion'. That can and does occur, of course – and not simply through shared experience of specific historical events, as Mannheim (1952) supposed, but more generally through the clash of tastes and perceptions adjusted to different successive states of the systems of goods and opportunities available (Bourdieu, 1993c: 99ff; on rock music, cf. Frith, 2007: 39; on shifts in the economic field, cf. Cohen, 1972). Children may also react and resist from an early age – as evidenced by all the more or less noisy little refusals to eat, dress, behave, etc., as parents demand (see Grieshaber, 2004) – and this can be exacerbated or spurred, as we will see in the next chapter, by a variety of factors. Indeed, players defined as 'children' can even, especially within the domestic subspace, become the dominant players in some cases, with parents feeling dominated, bullied or threatened by their offspring in different ways depending on the distribution of all capitals operative within the field.

On top of gender and generation, finally, a few further factors specify the structure and struggles of particular family fields. These include (as already hinted) *class* difference, even if weighted by the social capital *qua* proxy capital generated by consociation, and *ethnic/national* differences, both of which can produce conflicting perceptions of the possible, the 'done thing' and the desirable thing. The clash of Bourdieu's own parents – a poorly paid and politically radical father and a déclassé mother with a concern for respectability (Bourdieu, 2007: 84–90) – is an instance of the former, while Beck and Beck-Gernsheim (2014) trawl many examples of national differences in conceptions of appropriate gender relations, expressions of love, 'good taste' and so on generating struggle and conflict between family members. *Number of children* (itself the product of fertility strategies) and *birth order* may also have their effect, generating very different strategies of capital investment (having to invest everything in a single child or in multiple children) and extra space for struggles within the field for recognition ('sibling rivalry') including through inheritance of economic and symbolic artefacts (Finch and Mason, 2000). *Trajectory* may also play a role, not just in terms of the life course or shifts in relative power of each member, but covering all the possible ruptures and evolutions of the familial field as a whole such as death, separation, re-partnering and reconstitution. For example, new agents with a specific perceptual status ('step', 'half'), sometimes importing their own doxic practices and attitudes, can be brought into the field, generating, in some instances, clashes, contradictions and resistance ('that's not how my mum did it', 'you don't know me!', etc.) (Allan et al., 2011).

Sometimes, where masculine and/or parental domination is absolute, it is possible that the power relations within the familial field come to function in a manner akin to what Bourdieu referred to, in a pretty offhand, undeveloped and hesitant reference to Althusser and Luhmann, like an 'apparatus' (Bourdieu and Wacquant, 1992: 102; cf. Bourdieu, 1998: 70), though since there are still dominant and dominated parties and nearly always some measure of resistance and struggle, no matter how small, even in these cases that only really describes a certain *state* of field relations rather than the absence of a field. In any case some might argue that, historically speaking, the move from more 'traditional' forms of partnering and childrearing towards the (class-refracted) kinds of relationships described by Giddens (1992) and Beck and Beck-Gernsheim (1995, 2002) in 'late modernity' has brought the shaking of old power bases and the emergence of new ones, the contestation of once-ingrained patterns of dominance and the intensification or 'excitation' of struggle and resistance (on changes within Algerian families, cf. Bourdieu, 1979: 48). That may be so, but it should not be forgotten that there is plenty of evidence of struggle and contention among sets of agents united by common familial or domestic perceptual-linguistic constructions (whatever the appellation and content: *familias, oikos,* clan, etc.) throughout Western history, especially (given the bias of the records) among propertied or powerful agents for whom honour and inheritance – including of kingdoms and empires – were at stake (on ancient Rome, for example, see Dixon, 1992: 138ff; and on the dynastic state, Bourdieu, 2014). Certainly it is likely that the distribution of symbolic capital and power within familial fields follows different principles, or the same principles to different degrees, nowadays. It is entirely possible, for example, that specifically affective recognition, love as a capital, has taken on greater prominence in structuring familial struggles – and within individual lifeworlds vis-à-vis other fields and capital – in two stages. The first was an initial elevation of importance following the social changes underpinning the emergence of the sentimental nuclear family recounted earlier, followed by a second, more recent intensification of its prominence with the rise of professions centred on the definition, regulation and media presentation of emotional wellbeing and affective relations (Bourdieu, 1984; cf. Illouz, 2012). Through film, TV, magazine and internet presence, they have managed to foreground romantic/parental love as a (or the) primary form of recognition towards which libidos should be channelled, to different degrees depending on other social positions occupied, and provide fictitious or embellished models of how it is/should be won and expressed against which reality can be (unfavourably) measured.

Boundaries, universes and constellations

But who, exactly, are implicated in these struggles, and how does that square with the foundational premise that 'the family' is a category of thought and perception? Here we come to an issue that has long vexed sociologists of the family – *boundaries* – but the solution here is very much the same as for any field. First of all, boundaries are themselves often a stake in the struggle within the field (Bourdieu and Wacquant, 1992: 100), so that, just as struggles over what counts and does not count as art or literature take place in the fields of cultural production (Bourdieu, 1996a), so too those within family fields can hold different views on who is and is not a legitimate player: children, for example, who no longer perceive their absent fathers as 'family' (see O'Brien et al., 1996), or who refuse to accept a step-parent or sibling as 'real' family, others who see lodgers or nannies as so woven into the routines, emotion and world of the family – into the doxa in other words – that they are perceived as 'like a daughter' or 'like a sister' and treated as such, and so on (cf. Bourdieu, 1990b: 172).[4] That said, and contrary to the quasi-ethnomethodological literature on 'doing' and 'displaying' families (Morgan, 1996; Finch, 2007) and the 'family boundaries' approach kicked off by Walker and Messinger (1979) and influential to this day (Allan et al., 2011: ch. 4), the *objective* structure of the field need not correspond with the perceptions with which competing members overlay it but is, of course, an empirical question hinging on the *detection of reciprocal effects* on dispositions and family doxa. So, for example, legal dissolution of marriage, physical dispersion of the family and even (or especially) fierce rejection of one another do not indicate the termination of the pertinent field effects but merely their evolution, whilst on the other hand the effects of certain members can become weaker and weaker until they are no longer really in the field at all, even if their residue lives on in the fact that the present state of the field will always owe its structure to its past.

So what, then, of all those agents *outside* of routine practice, beyond a specific familial doxa and field of relations of force, who are nevertheless described in folk discourse as 'family' through blood or marriage and who undoubtedly have some mediated or partial impact upon the agents within that family field, their habitus and perception of the possibles and so on by virtue of their linkages with particular agents within the field? And what then of the fact that agents can stand in different objective and subjective relations to one another (one person's close 'daughter' is another's distant 'aunt') such that they may be in more than one family field at a time? Again the solution comes from analogy with fields of cultural production, albeit one based on a particular reading of Bourdieu: just as the various national fields of music production or of sociology might not have added up to a unified 'global field' twenty or so years ago (today might be different) but instead formed what he rather elliptically referred to as a 'universe' of interpenetrating homologies, influences (mediated we would add, by networks and circuits of symbolic power), and multiple field memberships (see e.g. Bourdieu, 1991), so too do the almost infinitely overlapping family fields. Admittedly he sometimes used the term universe synonymously with field, but we can accord it a particular, distinct conceptual status.

This means that the effects of more (experientially) distant kin may ripple through the universe via double-placed agents: the dispositions and actions of particular individuals (aunts, uncles, cousins or whatever) may impact on a given agent through their influence on the individuals who are members of both fields, perhaps through stories or gossip about family members, the meaning of which is determined vis-à-vis the familial doxa and its contestation (confirmation, modification, alternative models, shock and outrage, etc.), or just the fact that that mediating agent's dispositions and strategies in one field are inevitably shaped by their dispositions and strategies in the other. The main point is that, just as with any field, the impacts from the wider universe are translated into the internal logic of the local family field, and that – mirroring the situation with cultural and intellectual production, in which the US has been dominant since the mid-twentieth century – some regions of the universe are more dominant, with greater 'gravity' or 'weight', and thus more influential over local field conditions, than others. The only analytically significant difference is that the familial universe is comprised of much smaller-scale fields than the universes of cultural production, yet still extends, in its own configuration, over the worldwide web of human affective bonds, meaning that while the chain of mutual influences can, in theory, be traced almost indefinitely, it is the scholar's task to identify, 'on paper', the pertinent *constellations* of fields for the research question at hand, that is to say, the cluster of family fields with empirically significant mutual, if uneven, effects on one another. The difference between a family field and such constellations is not, it must be stressed, the same as that between 'close' and 'extended kin', for, returning to Bourdieu's vision of the family field in terms of the system of relations 'constantly reused' and reinforced in *practice* whatever the nominal status of individuals, so-called 'extended' kin may well share field membership whilst supposedly 'close' kin, as discussed above, may not.[5]

The two faces of family

Such are the parameters of family relations seen as a field. Current discourses of 'family', weaving through time and space along particular circuits of symbolic power, are embedded within a multitude of social struggles, centralized within the field of power and homologous with class, gender, the ethnic space and so on. They are 'realized' in everyday practice as specific individuals mutually orient on this basis but also resisted and modified in line with the social positions they occupy. And while reciprocal typification and a shared sense of what is done, or doxa, is fundamental to that realization and mutual orientation, so too is contention and domination in relation to the capacity to speak on what is or should be done, flowing from multiple forms of misrecognition of which love and care are paramount. If families have what might be called their Platonic face, their semblance of solidarity and mutual care, since the author of *The Republic* suggested the guardians of the ideal city-state use family terms when addressing one another (brother, sister and so on) in order to foster unity, cohesion and harmony between them; they also have their Aristotelian face, their internal power-imbalances and struggles, since the peripatetic thinker was prone to liken kinship relations to the largest structures of socio-political subjugation.

However, while Bourdieu's logic has been necessary for grasping the constitution and generic structures of familial relations, and while it is indispensable to study those in themselves – the rancorous struggles to define 'family', the changing typical configuration of familial power relations in a social order and so on – to reap the full analytical benefit of conceiving the family as a field of struggle we must also go beyond his own customary approach. For just as important as the formation, maintenance and organization of a family field is the field's *relationship with other fields* in each implicated individual's lifeworld – whether of strain, clash, accord and so on, with interest and strategies in one playing positively or negatively into interest and standing in another. This has particular pertinence for grasping the rival pressures facing women nowadays in the wake of feminization of the workforce, as we will see in chapter 5, but it also counters those critics who deplore Bourdieu for ignoring the complicating role of family relations in channelling children's desires and trajectories, dissolving them into class relations or treating it as a mysterious 'black box' (e.g. Goldthorpe, 2007; Archer, 2012; Jaeger and Breen, 2013). To fully demonstrate that case, however, we now need to plunge more deeply into the intricate process through which we human beings each come to be who we are.

4

Social Becoming

The familial field may be the key to understanding how what we call 'social reproduction' is the product of the most intimate yet mundane relations, and even how, in some instances, it may go awry. Already, by building on some of Bourdieu's own sketchy remarks, we have seen the agency and desires of children and the complexity of the social relations in which they are enmeshed emphasized more than was his usual tendency. Yet we need to go further still, for Bourdieu's habitual talk of parent–child relations in terms of 'inculcation', 'transmission', 'conditioning', 'absorption', 'immersion', 'imbibing' and non-conscious imitation, while providing provocative metaphors or parsimonious means of making sense of statistical regularities, are – as others researching family life, schooling and child development have pointed out for decades – too blunt, too homogenizing and too quick to cast learning, and indeed social becoming more broadly, as a largely passive and automatic process (e.g. Connell, 1983; Cicourel, 1993; Morgan, 1999; Jenkins, 2002; Sayer, 2005; Goldthorpe, 2007; Archer, 2012; Corsaro, 2015). Children are active learners, engaging with their environment and others around them to build up not just bodily capacities and masteries but understandings of the world adjusted to the experiences they face. Which masteries and understandings they develop, in which specific fields large and small they opt to ply them and even their success in doing so, moreover, depend not only on the abstract 'pedagogic work' of parents and others but the specific structure of affective relations underpinning that work given by, first of all, the space of familial struggle and then, increasingly, the expanding mesh of field effects pervading the growing child's experience.

Bourdieu (2000b: 164–7) did, to be fair, gesture in this general direction in his later work, suggesting that the insights of sociology and psychology should be combined to document how an individual's desire and capacity to invest in any one social game is born of the earliest and ongoing childhood experiences. That, then, is precisely what I aim to do here: to embellish and put on firmer conceptual footing Bourdieu's suggestive account of the process through which concrete, empirical individuals come to be what they are, possess the masteries they do and yearn for what they do by not only drawing on what has been argued in previous chapters but integrating into it selected insights from the major traditions of developmental psychology. These traditions are Jean Piaget's 'genetic epistemology', Lev Vygotsky's 'sociocultural' approach and, of course, psychoanalysis. The task is complicated by the fact that the three are often seen as antagonistic towards one another and towards phenomenology, and each – particularly Piaget and psychoanalysis – has been described by different commentators as an unacknowledged foundation of, a critical counter for, or a necessary addition to Bourdieu's own thought. Lahire (2011), for example, implies that the habitus is nothing more than a sociological appropriation of Piaget's work anyway, while Lizardo (2004), more charitably, sees the Swiss psychologist as a fundamental, if subterranean, influence on Bourdieu, setting the latter at odds with phenomenology. Bronckart and Shurman (1999), on the other hand, recognize the link between Bourdieu and Piaget yet try to wrestle the habitus more towards the Vygotskian corner (see also Connolly, 2004). Others, meanwhile, have traced the ambivalent place of psychoanalysis in Bourdieu's work, noting his resistance to it – despite his own brief endorsements of 'object relations' theory (Bourdieu, 2000b: 166; 2001: 85) – and seeking to augment his tools with its distinctive concepts (Fourny, 2000; Steinmetz, 2006, 2014; George, 2014; Silva, 2016). Honneth (1996) too has tied his recognition-based philosophical anthropology to Bourdieu at the sociological end and object relations theory at the psychological end.

In fact, each perspective emphasizes different but complementary themes which, if extracted and viewed through the lens of relational phenomenology, can be combined to yield a sounder model of social becoming than that customarily found in the pages of Bourdieu's works. Piaget offers tools for reconstructing the genesis of practical and symbolic mastery, and more generally of the habitus, through experience and active practice *ab incunabilis*; Vygotsky embeds that process within socio-cultural relations, offering a means of connecting with sociological research to elaborate the genesis of class (and other) differences in forms of mastery; and psychoanalysis brings the missing puzzle pieces of desire and struggle into the mix. All three, however, remain hampered not only by specific oversights of what the other perspectives underscore but by an inadequate conception of social relations, familial relations prime amongst them, and here is where Bourdieu, and relational phenomenology, offer a corrective in return.

The Baseline(s)

The foundation upon which the proposed fusion will be built is the phenomenological conception of habitus proposed in chapter 1 and alluded to at various points hitherto. This, to recapitulate, foregrounds the horizons of perception, these being all that is co-given with perception of an (inner or outer) object, subject or event without actually being present in the sensory data. This includes the *temporal* horizon, i.e. expectation of the immediately forthcoming or possible, but also the elements of what might be called the *synchronic* horizon informing that: intuition of aspects of the object not directly perceived, practical awareness of the object's place within particular systems of relations (i.e. fields), and apperception of its pertinence *across* fields, or the world horizon.[1] The crucial question is how these horizons get to be 'filled in' as they are, accumulating and shifting over time for any one individual. The vocabulary of genetic phenomenology, as founded by Husserl (2001) and elaborated by Schutz (1972), puts it in terms of 'synthesis': in the course of experience certain properties, activities and sensations come to be associated or paired with certain objects/subjects/motor actions as typical and distinct from others, thence sitting in the horizons of perception of that object/subject/action. Synthesis can be passive – the simple, automatic, pre-predicative recording or 'sedimentation' of associations – or active – the explicit, conscious formation of a judgement as to association, with the association sinking into the horizon even if the original act of judgement is forgotten. Passive synthesis can, moreover, be primary – premised purely on the contents of individual experience – or secondary – communicated to oneself by others, and therefore more collective and communal in character. As any serious reader of Husserl will know, there is a vast and complex network of interconnected notions branching off from these distinctions, but these are the key elements of the story.

Yet emphasizing the phenomenological construction of the habitus is not quite enough on its own to provide a firm foundation for rethinking social becoming. From Husserl to Schutz, phenomenology misses, or at least has a very weak conception of, something which has featured in previous chapters but has, up to this point, been taken for granted: *desire*. Not how desire for specific objects comes to be constructed, which inevitably depends on processes of synthesis, but of how human beings are inherently desiring, striving beings, experiencing pleasure or lack thereof in relation to the world (see Atkinson, forthcoming a). For sure, we can recognize the notion shared by Bourdieu and phenomenology that the elements of the horizon active in perception at any one time, feeding into thematic thought, directing attention and guiding practice are generally based on the 'principle of pertinence' (Bourdieu, 1990b: 90) – selecting and filtering according to the formula of 'first things first' in relation to 'the matter at hand', which, Bourdieu emphasizes, generally revolves around the struggle for recognition. We have already established that there are *multiple* pertinences and 'matters at hand' competing for an individual's attention across time and space, and Schutz's (1970) work on why one thing becomes relevant to someone at one time and not another introduced the useful distinction between *imposed* pertinences – an external stimulus in the lifeworld (including the actions of others) forces us to turn our attention to something – and *intrinsic* pertinences – (re)turning from one theme to another without external stimulus. But why do humans find *anything* pertinent? Why are the matters at hand deemed imperative? What is the underpinning motor, or *condition of possibility*, of the quest for recognition? To answer this we need to integrate a notion from developmental psychology before we even get to the actual course of development: the *libido*. Taken from psychoanalysis, of course, Bourdieu always indicated this was key to grasping investment in the manifold games comprising social life, but his ambivalent relationship to Freud's legacy meant he never really elaborated on it (Steinmetz, 2014).

So how best to define the libido for our purposes given the multitudinous versions of the notion out there? First, the original Freudian model of libido, which Bourdieu (2000b: 166) himself seemed to subscribe to, is too narrow, being overly focused on sexuality – which is merely one aspect of desire rather than the foundation for all desire – and too tightly bound to a 'zonal determinism' working through distinct developmental stages (Chodorow, 1978: 66). Most attempts to rethink or redefine it, however, have proven to be similarly narrow and reductive but in different ways. Certainly this is the case with Bowlby (1969), whose effort to replace it with instinct to attach to a single caregiver ends up framing all development in terms of a restrictive attachment/loss binary, but also with Fairbairn's (1952) endeavour to redefine libido, in tune with object-relations theory, as an impulse to connect with others – which just so happens to be expressed orally to begin with since this is the 'path of least resistance' to others. As neat as it might seem for grounding claims for humanity's inherent sociality, the evidence is fairly scanty, premised on reading an awful lot into infant behaviour, and it implausibly reduces all pleasure-seeking (feeding, thumb-sucking, etc.) to person-seeking (Balint, 1956). Perhaps the most prudent position – despite all his untenable mysticism – is Jung's (1961, 1969) widening of the libido to encompass the generalized 'psychic energy', manifesting subjectively as desire, which can be channelled in different (multiple) directions in different proportions at different times and which can be blocked, dampened, height-ened or rechanneled depending on experience.[2] This cer-tainly brings it closer to the other term Bourdieu tended to use to render striving, desire, appetite and will, *conatus*, a borrowing from Spinoza, but (returning to the core meaning of the latter term in Latin) without the end necessarily being self-preservation. One may well desire or strive for self-destruction, for example, not as part of a drive separate from the libido as Freud supposed, but as the end to which psychic energy happens to have been channelled through experience.

Incorporating a broad definition of libidinal striving into a phenomenological reading of habitus necessitates that we recast what would normally be described as the activity of the 'unconscious', including what Jung and Lacan in particu-lar would call 'complexes', or tendencies to think or act a particular way in response to certain precipitants. Fleshing out Merleau-Ponty's (2014) accommodation of a 'broad' ren-dering of psychoanalysis with Schutz and Luckmann's (1973) discussion of 'attitudes' and 'syndromes' and their activation *in situ*, therefore, these should be seen as nothing more than the fringing of experience with a very particular horizon. An object/person/event is perceived automatically as a *type* of object/person/event, with a typical pattern of future activity yielding a sense of the likely forthcoming and laden with affective association insofar as it bears or has borne on the libido. It then activates typical chains of responsive activity which have, through processes of synthesis, been paired with the type of object/person/event as more or less effective in heightening pleasure or reducing tension/anxiety (experienced as an 'I must', 'it is stronger than me'). The genesis of this particular horizon and its motivating force – which Schutz (1972) described as the 'because motive' to distinguish it from the 'in-order-to motive' constituting the individual's *post-hoc* rationalization of why they did what they did (which can include so many 'biographical illusions', as Bourdieu [2000a] put it) – is generally beyond conscious thematization, not because of some active operation of repression, however, but because it is forged out of multiple experiences and unnoticed passive syntheses and, in many cases, because it occurs before the capacity for memory recapitulation has developed.

The early structuring of the habitus

Such are the abstract principles of motivation and habitus formation. Now we need to give them specific form by selectively assimilating the findings of developmental psychology to trace the progressive transformation of knowledge, dispositions and desire from our earliest days. The first thing to note is that the infant is not born as a *tabula rasa*, thrust into a world of sheer 'blooming, buzzing confusion' as James (1950: 488) put it, but imposes perceptual structures from the outset. There are two reasons for this. The first is the nature of the human mind: research has shown that newborn infants are predisposed to attend to edges, borders and sharp contrasts (door frames, wall corners, chess boards, etc.) (Haith, 1980), and the inference is that this is because the human mind is geared to *distinguish* and *differentiate* – to slowly but surely carve up the visual field into distinct entities, set in relation to one another (up/down, left/right, near/far, whole/part, light/dark), which can become thematic or peripheral in consciousness (Merleau-Ponty, 2014). Second, a vast catalogue of scholarship suggests that the earliest syntheses of experience occur, and thus the very first perceptual horizons are formed, *in utero*. Newborn infants, for example, have been shown to recognize and display a preference (insofar as familiarity is comforting) for the sounds and voices that have become familiar during gestation, and particularly the voice of the mother, which is audible from the womb and then paired with the mother's face postpartum (DeCasper and Fifer, 1980; Kisilevsky et al., 2003). Even rooting for and suckling at the mother's breast – which might be considered 'the most natural thing in the world' – is the product of a passive synthesis of pre-natal experience: the infant is drawn to the nipple, and sucking triggered, because the odour the nipple secretes resembles that of amniotic fluid, the intake and swallowing of which *in utero* the infant has come to associate with having a full stomach (Porter and Winburg, 1999). There is also some debate, drawing on research on neonate imitation and interaction with caregivers, over whether we are oriented towards others from the start, and thus inherently social and intersubjective (Meltzoff and Moore, 1977; Gopnik et al., 1999; Trevarthen and Aitken, 2001), but the evidence is patchy and prone to being overblown (Welsh, 2013), with no conclusive confirmation that the special attention newborns give to other people is not the product of the first syntheses and generalizations of postnatal experience (mother's voice → mother's face → others' faces). Nevertheless, it does seem humans are picked out as particularly interesting entities within the visual field, entwining with the tendency to differentiate, from the very start. This is not yet a struggle for recognition – that comes later – but it is its first foundation.

Once out in the world the infant begins to build and refine schemas of typification and opposition. Initially, and for a long while, synthesis, horizon-filling and capacity ('I can') formation occur, as Piaget (1977) argued, on the *sensory-motor plane*, unmediated by the use of symbols or signs. At first these are organized around the activity of sucking, since the mouth, under the infant's control like nothing else yet and the route to satisfaction (stimulation/tension release), is the principal tool of exploration at this stage. Through the repeated experience of feeding the infant hones sets of motor actions adapted to success in satisfying its desire, becoming more dexterous at feeling and grasping by accommodating different textures, sights and movements, and comes to associate certain bodily postures with certain experiences (starting or stopping feeding) such that they call forth certain actions (e.g. oral search for the nipple). These first dispositions are laced with affect too, as consistent positive or negative experience in relation to the breast/bottle (e.g. not feeding enough or quickly enough) tinges subsequent perception and protention with emotional charge. Here, of course, is where psychoanalysts would locate the beginnings of the unconscious, with Melanie Klein (1932) in particular highlighting the effects of the infant's transition from seeing the breast/bottle/caregiver as distinct 'good objects' and 'bad objects' from situation to situation depending on the particular experience to a single permanent object characterized by both positive and negative traits – a claim which chimes with Piaget's thesis that infants start to develop a sense of general object permanence after the first few months of life. The phenomenological reading of the habitus 'flattening' the depth model of personality associated with the unconscious into the horizons of perception, however, casts this in a specific way. The nipple/teat/caregiver, or associated objects and activity, is, as Merleau-Ponty (2014) had it, simply fringed with a halo of greater or lesser *ambivalence* depending on the nature of experience over time, the full genesis of which is inaccessible to conscious reconstruction later only because it occurs before the ability to reconstruct memories has developed. The latter depends on manipulation of symbols and, as Paul Ricoeur famously explored and Bourdieu (2000a) specified, linguistic, narrative reconstruction – capacities which, as we will see, only come later.

Soon enough the infant begins to master bodily movements and capacities, organized around carnal oppositions
of up/down, left/right, fast/slow and so on, and fill in the
horizons of perception through activity (including direct imitation of others) not ostensibly related to – and sometimes
in competition with – the urge to suck. The latter is still the
prime channel for desire and the principle of pertinence, for
sure, but the mastery of the 'moderately novel' in the environment (in Piaget's words) also draws a portion of the libido
when it is relatively satisfied. At the same time the child is
expanding their bank of pre-symbolic perceptual associations and distinctions regarding objects in the world. To
convey this – and furnishing a more differentiated account
of perceptual horizons – Piaget borrows, but usefully speci-
fies, Saussure's distinction between the signifier (that which
stands for, or represents, something else) and the signified
(the something else which is being represented). In this period
the signifier, not clearly disentangled from the signified,
takes the form of a 'signal' or 'indication', i.e. a sensory
impression of an object which automatically points to other
qualities associated with the object through experience, particularly typical chains of future activity. A bib, for example,
or more specifically the experience of having a bib put on,
is associated with forthcoming feeding and calls forth both
an affective response and the set of associated motor schemas
in readiness or (if the infant is not hungry, teething, etc.)
resistance. Signals thus underpin the first grasp of *classes* of
stimuli and their inter-relationships, as certain impressions
are grouped as alike and paired with certain bodily schemas
(and necessarily opposed to others), as well as the first perceptions of the imminent future and the possibilities for
action they indicate.

From here into the first few months of life, shows Piaget,
the child begins to coordinate her capacities, refine her corporeal schema and expand the sense of the possible. Motor
masteries that were previously separate – the schemas of
looking (focus, eye movements, head control, recognition of
increasingly diverse objects), hearing (differentiating direc-

tions and varieties of sound) and grasping, for example –
begin to work together and become refined so that the infant
can complete more complex and temporally extended chains
of action, such as grasping something making a noise in
order to look at it or suck it. This does not, as some of
Bourdieu's language might sometimes suggest, occur simply
through passive synthesis, however, but through pre-symbolic
active synthesis too. As Piaget documented, the very young
infant is actively, intentionally engaging with her environment to bring about certain ends and exploring the capacities
of her body. From grasping and sitting to crawling, she is
concentrating and experimenting, which is to say that mobilizing and mastering postures and movements become *thematic*, whether as a means to a certain goal – recreating
pleasurable or interesting events, reaching a toy/parent, etc.
– or as ends in themselves.

Of course the background to all of this, as otherwise
diverse strands of psychoanalysis collectively demonstrate, is
a basic degree of security, trust in the world and routine for
the infant, and here, along with the development of schemas
around feeding already mentioned, is where other people –
mostly absent from Piaget's analysis – tend to figure at this
stage. Experience of the caregivers' care over time – or more
accurately, association of specific human faces, smells, etc.,
with consistent relief of discomfort, hunger, boredom, etc.,
on crying – produces not only a more or less positive halo
of associations on perception of the caregivers, soliciting
certain responses (e.g. smiles), but, in Erikson's (1977: 222)
words, 'inner certainty' and 'outer predictability', or we
might say, 'horizontal' awareness that the infant is safe, that
they will be tended to if needed even if the caregiver is not
presently perceived and that they can get on with exploring
the world and their bodies. Negative or inconsistent experience in this regard, which is common enough to some degree
for most infants (who cannot yet communicate their precise
woes after all), but which may also take more extreme forms,
is also synthesized into typifications of the situation and
the caregivers, however, contributing again to the greater or

lesser sense of ambivalence that fringes perception of others and potentially leaving a lasting sediment of generalized anxiety and mistrust.

This is still not, to begin with at least, a struggle for or sense of lack of recognition from the caregiver, however, since that depends on specific developments that come a little later. The same cannot necessarily be said for the caregivers or others within the family field, however. At the same time as they are continuously building and revising their own typifications of the infant's behaviour and how to adjust to it (shaped by and reshaping to some degree existing ideas of childrearing drawn from the media, the medical field, family lore and so on), they may well seek justification for their existence not just 'as a mother/father/etc.' but directly through the infant's smiles, laughs and so on.[3] This will shape their practice in relation to the child – being more or less attentive, protective, etc. – and even have distinct effects on the structure of the field as a whole, generating jealousy, greater love or a mix thereof from other players, for example. Indeed it has to be borne in mind that deciding to have (or keep) a child is not just a classed project in the manner suggested by Bourdieu (1998: 69; 2000b: 165) – as a way to further the family's trajectory – but *a strategy within the family field*, contextualized by the forces of the field as a whole as well as the balance of forces between the fields shaping one's lifeworld. It could be an effort to compensate for a more or less consciously perceived lack of love or esteem from others – a lowly position in the field – by generating a being (a player) expected to love and/or obey oneself, or to demonstrate love for or secure love/commitment from another in the field, or to make a virtue of necessity and find a route to recognition (as a parent) if movement through work-related fields and the social space is blocked, and so on. The creation and nurturance of human beings is in no way divorced from plays for symbolic capital and the powers it can bring.

This is, in fact, just one way in which the infant, though not yet at this stage a full player within a specific field, is still shaped by fields. The way in which their caregivers respond to them and attend to their needs, and perhaps even try to actively 'train' their motor skills, but also their accents, the household division of labour, the sights, sounds and aromas around the house and all the chains of activity linking them together not only bear the stamp of their parents' and wider family's social positions – their class tastes, their ethno-racial habitus and their gendered dispositions – but are enmeshed within wider circuits of symbolic power. All of these feed into the first motor skills and categorizations of the world, the first signals and expectations, even *in utero*, generating a distinct sense of the 'normal', 'typical' and 'familiar' – and thus, to a degree, the comforting – as well as, in contrast, the abnormal, impossible and alien. The child is born socially differentiated, no matter how minimally, and the specific lifeworld she finds herself thrust into means even the most basic capacities and categorizations she forms to deal with it at first, constituting the filter through which all subsequent experience is sifted, are inflected with an idiosyncratic hue.

The struggle begins

Between six and 18 months old, however, the struggle for recognition on the infant's behalf finally begins. This is because this is the period in which they go through *the mirror stage*, famously described by Lacan (1977/2001) and taken up by Merleau-Ponty (2014). The infant has already begun to be aware of the reflection of the caregiver – fringed with affective horizons and the indirect object of desire insofar as the infant desires that they tend to her needs – in a mirror. Now, however, she begins to realize, through the caregiver's encouragement and approval of their response to the specular image,[4] two things: first, that she is a separate, distinct being, an object in the world perceived by others, and second, that those others are experiencing, desiring subjects like her. This is the birth of intersubjectivity proper, insofar as subjectivity like one's own is now appresented with perception of the other's body, but also, with this, the birth of a sense of 'self' or 'ego' which can be taken as the theme of consciousness, both adding up to the state of human being as *being-perceived* (Bourdieu, 2000b: 166).[5] The infant is able to see the world through the eyes of others, that the indirect objects of desire – caregivers – are desiring beings with a point of view, that the infant can herself be an object of desire and that caregivers tend to their needs on this basis. Consequently – and in tandem with the linguistic injunctions mentioned in the previous chapter – the original libido, initially directed towards any object bringing satisfaction (breast/bottle/fingers), is now channelled directly towards caregivers. More specifically, the infant begins to desire that they be their object of desire's object of desire – or more simply, as Kojève (1969) put it, they desire the other's desire – and this involves acting, talking and thinking in ways which will win their esteem, care and love, and thus deliver certain powers ('getting what one wants'). There is, therefore, the emergence of a first *illusio*, a first *capital* and the first *strategies* aimed at accruing or maintaining it – in other words, the child becomes immersed in their first *field*. The greater or lesser ambivalence fringing perception of others, meanwhile, is imbued with a fresh significance as it comes to be paired in perception with a desiring subjectivity both granting and withholding recognition.

The pertinent relational web here is not, it must be stressed, the classic mother–baby dyad of the various branches of psychoanalysis – whether object-relations theory, Lacanian structuralism or attachment theory – nor even the Oedipal triad, since that is to remain stuck at the level of substantial, interpersonal, interactive relations. Even those psychoanalysts factoring in the effect of siblings on struggles for affective recognition (as competitors but also colluders) do not go far enough (e.g. Mitchell, 2003). Sure enough, the domestic sub-space takes on particular pertinence given the generalized doxa and spatial (household) organization of familial relations in contemporary Western societies, but the genetic principle of all practices in the first struggle for recognition is *the structure of the family field as a whole.* The ways in which individuals within the field act towards the infant, including parents, and thus the degree of recognition they impart to her – included through the level of in/dependence and autonomy granted or encouraged, responses to cries, gestural and verbal interaction and labelling (pet names, insults) and such like – are shaped by the position of each within the distribution of familial powers and their degree of submission to the familial *illusio.* A parent's interaction with their child only makes full sense, in other words, when the full space of affective power relations, incorporating – most likely – their own parents, partners and others (including the doting or stern nannies and wet nurses that pervade many psychoanalytic cases), *and* their trajectory over time (a fall from favour, a lost child, etc.), are factored in, as these shape the perception of what can, should and must be done in the more or less banal, subtle, daily struggles for love.

This shift in perspective from dyad/triad to field not only allows accommodation of cross-cultural and historical variation in the constitution and content of childrearing and familial struggles, a known weak spot of psychoanalysis, but also throws fresh light on many of the so-called 'defence mechanisms' postulated by Freud and catalogued by his daughter (Freud, 1968). For if the field structure provides not only adults but infants with a *sense of place* within it vis-à-vis others – subordination, difference and similarity to others, etc. – and thus a *field of possible actions,* then what are these defences if not collections of practices, sometimes becoming dispositional over time and transposed into other fields via 'analogical transfer' (Lahire, 2011), aimed at maintaining recognition given the state of play and the relatively limited range of moves for the young child? For example, whereas 'reaction-formation' for Freud is a defensive inversion in consciousness of unconscious, instinctual drives, from the point of view of relational phenomenology it can be understood as an attempt to subvert elements of the field and its doxa by turning against those objects, people or practices associated with negative experiences – producing anxiety, stress, pain and such like – flowing from a dominated position within the field, i.e. *symbolic violence* (which may well be accompanied by physical violence). Similarly we can recast 'negation' (*Verneinung*) as denial of the existence of an event, trait, etc., potentially diminishing familial/ affective recognition, 'projection' as appresenting aspects of one's self threatening a loss of capital onto others, 'introjection' as the imitation of traits of dominant others in the field to win familial esteem, and 'regression' as returning to earlier practices paired with ready recognition to counter perceived lack of recognition in the present. Moreover, 'idealization' of others outside the field is not simply the artefact of a drive amongst girls to solve the lack of perceptual differentiation of self from mother, as it is for Chodorow (1978: 137), but a more widespread product and producer of the struggle against the orthodox construction of 'what is done' and 'what is right' within the familial field.

Mastery, pedagogy and love

By the age of two the child is going through toilet training, and the way in which parents handle this – with disgust, pride, calmness, anger, etc. – leaves a lasting impression insofar as the child finds ways to deal with the recognition or lack of recognition it signifies. If parental disgust generates a particularly 'anal' disposition, as Freud claimed, it is only because the latter constitutes the lasting sediment of a strategy to avoid the shame and fear experienced by the infant desiring her parents' love, i.e. to maintain standing given the structure of the field and the limited possibilities for the infant. More importantly, however, by two years old the child has, as Piaget (1977) examined, begun to be able to differentiate signifier and signified and supplement signals with use of *symbols.* They are, in other words, able to read in the perception of one sound, object, movement or mental image reference to something else, thus evoking that which is absent, even if those signifiers are related by evident resemblance to the signified – an imitative sound or movement, a picture, etc. The signified in this instance tend to be what Piaget (1962) dubbed 'preconcepts': unstable, mobile and idiosyncratic typifications of a class of objects or events which, by virtue of practical analogy and concrete comparison (so many operations of synthesis and association), are more generous or more restrictive than conventional use – a 'cat' as any animal with four legs, for example, or as animals with four legs, tail, etc., and which are also always black. Although there is little in the way of consistent wider logic about the how the world works, the child is also now able to discover new means to attain a goal by way of mental combination, i.e. thought (their own potential practice becoming thematic in the mind's eye) rather than physical, sensory-motor practice, and to imitate absent models by actively reconstructing their activity.

Eventually, however, the child begins to master the final form a signifier can take: the *sign*, an abstract and arbitrary image-sound couplet whose meaning is conventionally, collectively determined, words and numbers being the prime examples. At the same time the signified are more likely to harden into 'concepts' – stable typifications premised on the classification of properties around whole-part relations, including of one's 'self' ('that's not me'). Although Piaget does not dwell on it, he admits that symbols and signs, like motor schemas, are always defined relationally. In his own words, the mind is not in the business of forming 'relations of identity', or 'static affirmation of identity' – which might be read as rejections of substantialism – but of distinguishing terms, differentiating them and organizing them into 'totalities' comprised of relations of 'reciprocity' (Piaget, 1977: 276). Concepts and their signs, preconcepts and symbols, indications and their signified derive their significance in relation to what they are not, or what they are opposed to, which is picked up through repeated practical experience. Moreover – and here we break with Piaget, who falsely depicts meaning as innocent and universal across society – while signs and concepts may well have some collective or conventional dimension within a social order, rendering their meaning *doxic*, we must insist that (i) the meaning of even the most apparently universal signs and concepts has been forged and imposed through multiple social struggles and circuits of symbolic power, and that (ii) each person will still develop their own *particular point of view on them* depending on their social position – a 'cat' is co-given with a sense of disgust or delight depending on class taste, for example, or invested with particular significances and associations in cultural and economic fields (media/artistic/ advertising/industry depictions). There are, in other words, dominant and dominated, orthodox and heterodox and field- and strategy-specific horizons to even the most basic words, numbers and concepts, albeit built on a base of shared doxic meaning.

Coinciding with the growing mastery of symbols and signs, argues Piaget, the child begins to reason about how the world works. By the age of seven or eight they are conducting 'concrete operations', that is to say, operations of classifying, arranging, adding/subtracting and so on, but only in relation to objects and events directly perceived or relevant to practical experience, and then, by adolescence, 'formal operations', in which the same operations can be conducted in relation to abstract or hypothetical objects, events, ideals and sign systems like those of mathematics or logic (see Piaget and Inhelder, 1969). The transition from the sensory-motor stage to concrete operations, and from there to formal operations, is characterized by what Piaget called 'vertical lag', or the fact of being able to do something using schemas of an earlier stage which one has not yet developed appropriate schemas for in a later stage – being able, for example, to achieve on the sensory-motor plane, in action, something without being able to conceive it using concepts or to articulate it using signs; or being able to solve in everyday life a problem which if put to the child abstractly would confound them.

What Piaget is imperfectly describing here is, in fact, the difference between practical mastery and symbolic mastery established by Bourdieu and Passeron (1990). To clarify, practical mastery covers several modes of competence unified by a certain style. First there is parsimonious mastery and mobilization of the signs constituting the mother tongue for efficient communication. Second, there is practical proficiency in logical relations insofar as they relate to everyday experience, like the young Brazilian street vendors studied by Carraher et al. (1988), or the fishermen studied by Schliemann and Nunes (1990), who can quickly carry out complex mathematical operations in relation to specific sales and haul weights in their heads but are unable to complete written sums. Sometimes, finally, there are refined sensory-motor capacities, in which the body, attuned through practice, efficiently unfolds chains of motor activity in response to specific varieties of stimuli – 'knowledge by hand' but also, in some cases, sporting or pugilistic prowess. Symbolic mastery, on the other hand, is the capacity to manipulate explicit formalizations of the principles of practice, whether grammar in relation to language, mathematical notation and operations in relation to arithmetic, abstract scientific concepts in relation to physical and social reality, or the history of art in relation to artworks. Ultimately this involves mastery of specific abstract sign and symbol systems, allowing one to not only identify and classify a formula, artwork, theory, etc., relative to others within an overall totality, but to interpret the most banal activities, objects and events of everyday life as exemplars of transcendent laws and tendencies. While logically coming after and being based on practical mastery developmentally, the acquisition of symbolic mastery transforms practice insofar as it at first nurtures 'conscious and systematic' adherence to (and interest in) those principles and sign systems (Bourdieu and Passeron, 1990: 46) only for that adherence and interest to become rather less conscious over time as they simply fade into the horizons of perception.

Yet Bourdieu and Passeron's point was that the different masteries, though co-existing to different degrees from individual to individual, correspond more or less with different parental class positions. The dominated are more likely to display, focus on and refine practical mastery, whereas those whose parents are rich in cultural capital tend to wield symbolic mastery to a greater degree, and this fact in turn reproduces social position insofar as practical mastery is only convertible into capitals garnering a lesser quantum of misrecognition – like physical capital or technical capital – while symbolic mastery is ultimately transformed via the education system into cultural capital, a more potent source of misrecognition. Piaget's error, then, is to *present as universal the developmental path of a specific class of children*, thus measuring other children's development unfavourably against it (cf. Donaldson, 1978; Walkerdine, 1984). He assumed scholastic reason and logical logic – his own modes of knowing the world – to be the apex of human intellectual development rather than an arbitrary principle of misrecognition, and found his views confirmed only because his test subjects were nearly always, as he himself admitted (Piaget, 1972: 6), from schools in Switzerland serving families possessing ample cultural capital. They were, therefore, already predisposed to succeed on the kinds of highly abstract exercises – usually based on physics, and utterly divorced from the practice and practicalities of everyday life – he made them do to measure their 'formal operational' logic.

This inevitably points to another failing of Piaget's account alluded to earlier: his determination to ignore or downplay the role *other people* play in shaping the masteries and the general horizons of young people, particularly family members (see Bruner and Haste, 1987). For the most part Piaget's child is a lone investigator, discovering the world through solitary experimentation and primary synthesis. When others do figure, other than as models of motor activity to imitate, it is via a limited interactionist conception of social relations in terms of exchanges of meaning to produce consensus (see Kitchener, 1991), leading him into the error of overlooking the differentiation of meaning already highlighted and to a weak conception of parent–child relations in terms of 'unilateral authority' blooming eventually into more or less harmonious 'democracy' (Piaget, 1932). Developmental psychologists uneasy with this asocial depiction of the child have tended to turn to Vygotsky (1978, 2012) to counter it. His view was that – at least after the sensory-motor phase of development – it was *mainly through* other people (and thus secondary synthesis) that children develop not only their preconcepts and concepts (which even Piaget admitted are constantly modified by the child asking others 'what's that?' and 'why?') but their modes of reasoning, or mastery, too, as adults – typically parents – suggest ideas, solutions and ways of thinking, and encourage recall of previous discoveries when the child is faced with a practical or abstract problem to solve. Even more subtly, there is evidence – usually huddled under the label of 'social referencing' – that infants from around one year old, when faced with an unfamiliar event, object or idea, will look specifically to caregivers to gauge their emotional response to it (e.g. happiness, anger, fear, sadness, etc.) before responding likewise (Feinman, 1992).

Bourdieu and Passeron (1990), of course, added in that the kind of explicit and implicit 'pedagogic work' done by parents differs according to their class position, giving substance to Vygotsky's otherwise vague interactionist account of social relations, and a whole raft of subsequent research has filled in the details (e.g. Tizard and Hughes, 2002; Lareau, 2003). Because of their practical mastery and daily experience of relative necessity, the dominated tend to ignore or give clipped responses to what/why questions since they find them difficult, talk primarily about domestic/family/money (i.e. concrete, everyday, practical) matters with their children, use language economically, play physical games (like tickling or chasing), make explicit pedagogy a separate, formal occasion distinct from 'fun', and generally let children do their own thing as 'they're only young once'. Those rich in cultural capital, on the other hand, tend to give elaborate answers to what/why questions, demand full and explicit verbalizations and elaborations from children (i.e. the making explicit of the principles of practice) in return, talk about abstract events and issues, correct grammar, take part in imaginative games and weave pedagogy into play.

Distinction also painted a rich picture of the milieus into which children in different classes are immersed, and the kinds of parental reactions to various cultural and political objects and events they are likely to encounter and 'reference' (Bourdieu, 1984).

As valuable as these corrections to Piaget's account are, however, there is still something missing. Both Vygotsky's psychology *and* Bourdieu and Passeron's early theory of reproduction lack a means of making sense of *why* children imitate, listen to, attend to the reactions of and talk and play with – but also why they resist – certain people rather than others, as well as why certain others want those children to imitate, listen to, heed and talk and play with them. There is, in short, no place for *desire*, whether on behalf of the children or the parents. In Vygotsky's case this flows from his Marxist, materialist view of language and knowledge as tools for the control of nature, but, as Merleau-Ponty (2014: 242ff) noted, it is impossible to separate the acquisition of signs, concepts and differential masteries from familial affect – in fact, we would add, *the latter is usually the flywheel for the former*. Returning to our sociologization of psychoanalysis, the development of practical and symbolic mastery are forged in the quest for recognition from those we misrecognize, that is to say, love and esteem from those we love or esteem, which is ultimately symbolic power in the eyes of those possessing symbolic capital in the field. Once the libido has been channelled toward the attainment of recognition within the familial/domestic field ('mummy, look at me!'), in other words, this in turn serves to channel portions of the libido towards other 'objects' – i.e. external capitals (physical, technical, cultural, artistic, etc.) and fields – insofar as different practices, utterances and projects appear to win affective capital in the form of congratulations ('well done!', 'good boy/girl!', 'you're so smart!'), hugs, smiles, rewards or even nods while others, including all the 'calls to order' that contribute to the sense of the possible and impossible fringing perception of certain goods or practices (*lusiones*),[6] threaten to deplete familial capital through indications of annoyance, anger or disappointment. The capital sought within the family is thus not simply another to add to the mix, *but a primal one shaping early misrecognition of and interest in accumulating any other.* Other capitals may well come to provide us with a reason for being, a justification for our existence in the face of finitude, and thus serve as their own ends, but our initial pursuit of non-familial capital is grounded in the original quest for recognition from caregivers, as means to another end.

This process, which might be taken as a sociological replacement for Freud's notion of sublimation, applies across the board – for level of investment and strategies in the ethno-racial/national field and sexual field (see chapter 5), for example. In terms of class and educational reproduction, however, the channelling of the libido – which surfaces in discourse in the guise of emergent 'passions', 'interests' or, as those influenced by Harry Frankfurt would have it (e.g. Archer, 2012), 'concerns' – towards accumulation of cultural capital through parental, institutionalized or self-directed pedagogy, or towards certain fields (e.g. of cultural production) with certain entry tickets (e.g. degrees, money, etc.), differs by possession of classed capitals within the familial or domestic field, its internal circulation and anticipations of the future built thereupon. In a nutshell, in family fields rich in pooled cultural capital, where there is a desire and – contingent on ongoing typifications of the child's growing mastery – expectation for offspring to more or less reproduce class position via the education system (on which cf. Devine, 2004; Irwin and Elley, 2013), attainment of affective capital from parents is doxically bound up with (*inter alia*) accumulation of symbolic mastery and thus cultural capital. In those less rich in cultural capital, with a different set of objectively likely and subjectively conceivable futures, it is less likely to be so – forms of practical mastery, including physical or technical capital, may be valued instead.

Now Bourdieu (2000b: 166–7) did move in this direction in his later work, seeing the familial field as the child's training ground for future field struggles, the first arena of contention in which 'investment in the social game', or the search for symbolic capital, is instilled. He even hinted at it as long ago as in *Distinction* (1984: 85). He was not so explicit and detailed, however, and, more importantly, he never systematically followed through on the full consequences of conceiving family relations as a field. For it may well be that in many, if not most, familial fields the doxa is policed firmly enough by parents presenting a 'united front' (Ribbens, 1994) to minimize struggle, channel the sense of possibles and search for recognition towards an (or multiple) endorsed field(s) and ensure a degree of social reproduction (Atkinson, forthcoming b). But in other fields there may be tension and contention between conservative orthodoxy and subversive heterodoxy producing *ambivalence towards* or even *rejection of inheritance*, and with it all kinds of deviant trajectories through the class structure, ethno-racial space, etc., as well as rebellious practices of consumption and position-taking. Subjection to warring familial views on the possible and desirable, born of distance within the social space, ethno-racial space and so on, or negative sentiment towards an overbearing parent – who is only as they are as part of a strategy for securing or maintaining recognition given the sum of their social positions, including within the familial field itself (vis-à-vis their own parents, for example) – can generate faltering and meandering pathways through formal education, defensive rejections of the specific cultural tastes, political attitudes or valued capitals of parents, and even rebellious valorization of paternally/maternally de-valorized external capitals ('I'll show them!') (Atkinson, 2011a, 2011b, 2012).[7]

Bourdieu (1996a: 10–12) did, it is true, recognize the possibility of this kind of ambivalence and conflict in his account of Frédéric Moreau, the protagonist of Flaubert's *Sentimental Education*, who equivocates between a career in law, politics and art, but – without wanting to attribute too much significance to the lives of fictional characters – his analysis was somewhat attenuated (cf. also Bourdieu, 2001: 70ff). Moreau, unlike his sometime antagonist de Cisy, the 'unproblematic heir', refuses not his inheritance but to be inherited by his inheritance, to 'get in line', take himself seriously and identify with the objectively probable future open to him. The source of this 'tergiversation' is, speculates Bourdieu, Frédéric's ambivalence towards his mother, who ceaselessly seeks to control his relationships (not least with his friend of lower standing, Deslauriers) and remind him of 'the imperatives of the worlds of business affairs and money', and a subsequent transfer of his love for his mother to Madame Arnoux, a potter's wife. Yet Bourdieu not only reduces Mme Moreau's relation with Frédéric down to a bald desire for her own 'social re-establishment' after a fall in social space, cleaving away her wish for Frédéric to succeed or 'settle' *because she cares for him*, which variously combines *and competes* with that wish for re-ascent (comforting him, accepting his decisions, etc.). He not only, in crude psychoanalytic vein, reduces Frédéric's ambivalence down to his mother's occupation of both feminine and masculine parenting roles given the premature death of her husband, which is no substitute for analysis of all the exchanges (even those within the novel) and strategies of mother and son (and others within the field such as uncle Barthélemy) establishing and maintaining the distribution of recognition in the field and feeding the ambivalent horizons. He also simplistically views the relation with Mme Arnoux as a case of Oedipal transfer rather than a subtle restructuring of the field and wider constellation of affective relations in line with the degree of recognition or symbolic power accorded to each player – temporarily diminishing, for example, the position of Frédéric's mother but not replacing it – and thus the erratic vacillation of young Moreau's libido.

Moreover, we can recast, and add further explicative padding to, Bourdieu's (1999c) discussion of the 'double bind' (a term borrowed from Gregory Bateson) or the 'contradictions of inheritance', that is to say, the struggles that arise in fulfilling parental hopes for social mobility. On the one hand, there are the paternal and maternal aspirations and expectations, acting as the domestic orthodoxy, which are grounded in the care and affection generated by the general family doxa and specified by the social positions and trajectories of both parents (including relative to one another and the other players within the family, which Bourdieu overlooks). The parents being bearers of symbolic capital within the field, these act as the source of affective capital for the child. Subsequent failure to match up to this aspiration, for whatever reason, produces parental disappointment, anger, shame, etc., to greater or lesser degrees, thus threatening affective capital, and this can generate defensive strategies within the field of the kind outlined earlier, including subversion in the form of reaction-formation or idealization of non-parental others, whether internal to the field (a grandparent, sibling, cousin, nanny, etc.) or, following the principle of heteronomy, external (a friend, teacher, political/media figure, etc.). More or less fulfilling the parental project, on the other hand, by ascending in the social space via the acquisition of cultural capital, may win affective capital in the form of pride and so on, but may also, paradoxically, destabilize it in other ways. Social distance may generate a divergence of lifestyle and ethos, a *sense* of distance ('I am not like you'), shame and embarrassment over each other's practices and even conflict over the right way to live (see Atkinson, 2015b: 14–17). This is negotiated differently in different familial fields depending on the state of play – sometimes it is more or less dissolved with humour, but occasionally it can cause serious rupture, revolution, denigration and suffering.

Integration into social space

Implicit in the foregoing – and in Bourdieu's (2000b) own account of social becoming – is an assumption worth making explicit and unpacking a little further: children are not born into a social space and its corresponding symbolic space. They inevitably affect their parents' and other family members' positions and strategies, not only insofar as they impact upon possession of economic, social and cultural capital – costing money, bringing new contacts and losing old ones, constraining entry into the education system, etc. – but insofar as the way they are dressed, fed, talked to and so on act as symbols to others of the parents' or family members' taste, ethos and positioning. Yet neonates and infants do not themselves start out as effective players in the social space because they have no investment in it, they have no 'sense of the game', they are not the agents of capitals and strategies and they are not recognized as such – they are not yet caught up in the field effects, in other words, even when they first become effective players in the familial field during the mirror stage. Evidently, through the circuits of symbolic power and resultant time-space paths of people and things, even young children constantly encounter not only concrete others in their lifeworld but also mediated others and their practices and products (via television or the internet, for example). This begins to feed into an incipient sense of the familiar and the possible, but at the same time *evaluation* of these others – their pertinence to the child's interests, that is – follows at first the original oral/mastery libido and then, later, the perceptual schemes forged in the familial field insofar as children reference their parents' or other family members' reactions (including those of the variety 'not for the likes of us') and judge them according to the state of play. From the very young child's point of view the family, the sole web of stable relations of recognition in which they are implicated, dominates lifeworld experience.

Over time, however, children are integrated into the social space and the symbolic space, opening out consciousness and desire from the closed world of the family alone to the wider topology of class relations. They come to misrecognize the capitals structuring the social space, and symbolized in the space of lifestyles, as legitimate, and either strive to acquire them or forge resistant strategies; they acquire a growing sense of the 'generalized other', as Mead (1934) had it, which is no more than a sense of one's place and a feel for the game, no matter how fuzzy; and they become recognized agents of capital, primarily *social* capital via their families at first, though with embodied and institutionalized cultural capital gaining salience over time. The family, as we have already seen, plays a crucial role in this process via the channelling of a portion of the child's libido towards non-familial objects as means to familial ends, but it does not play the only one. The education system (including pre-school) and the media field, via their circuits of symbolic power, are also key, pulling the child objectively and subjectively into the social and symbolic space by pushing them to situate the desires, doxa and positions of their caregivers and broader family field within a wider context, offering convergent or divergent models of legitimacy, difference and similarity ('people like me') – of how the world works and what it is comprised of – in line with the interests of the contenders within the national field of power, as well as stamping them with widely recognized markers of social worth in the form of educational qualifications. Disjunction between the familial message, conditions of existence and possibilities on the one hand, and the wider message and scholastic demands – comprising so many acts of symbolic violence if not 'symbolic annihilation', as Gerbner and Gross (1976) put it – on the other, can generate shame, embarrassment, self-consciousness and other manifestations of a sense of worthlessness, but also resistance and efforts of subversion. This much has been shown by generations of educational sociologists from Bourdieu and Passeron (1990) and Willis (1977) to Reay (2005).

There are, however, three complications and mediations to the integration process which, from the point of view of relational phenomenology and lifeworld analysis, cannot be ignored. The first is the dialectic between *time-space* location/ movement and the social/symbolic spaces. The implicit and explicit messages of the media field and education system, as fodder for secondary synthesis conducted through the lens of the family message, are already differentiated geographically by the spatio-temporal flows of people, things, ideas and resources extending out from players within the (inter) national and regional fields of power, local schooling provision being perhaps the most obvious example. On top of this, however, repeated experience of the kinds and conditions of buildings, vehicles, people and activities comprising the experiential fabric of the child's lifeworld not only give concrete substance to but also skew what is objectively probable and possible, and thus the sense of what is 'normal', 'likely', 'possible' and so on, the sense of one's place relative to others – and thus attachments to or desire to escape from place (Reay and Lucey, 2002; Stahl, 2015) – and what symbolizes or signifies social position (e.g. local fashions, slang and area names).

Take, for example, a child born to a family comprised of members of the dominant class living in a locale and attending a school disproportionately catering to the dominated. Immersed in a world suffused with the symbols and practices of the working class, they may experience a split between, on the one hand, the sense of where they stand in the wider picture as given by the measure of their own family-forged dispositions and discourse vis-à-vis the message from the media and the education system and, on the other, their sense of place relative to those encountered on a daily basis. While perhaps feeling they should be seen as worthy, since their tastes and orientations are officially lauded, they may be constantly denigrated ('teacher's pet'), bullied and shunned in lifeworld experience, bearing the brunt of the resistance of the dominated class in the symbolic struggle (see e.g. Sales, 2012). Or it might be that when they do come to be among those more socially proximate but experientially distant they feel different, with a different view on the world – perhaps more likely to see themselves as 'working class', for example – and having faced different *localized* symbolic struggles on a daily basis. Not only that, but this specific spatio-temporal ordering of the lifeworld – site and motility – differentiate the field of possibilities as, for instance, some activities otherwise associated with their position (like visiting art galleries regularly) may simply not be available locally.

Second, and following on from the last point, integration into social space is also specified by a dialectic with emerging *social networks*, the most significant of these for the young child being friendship networks. First of all, the pool of people young children are likely to become friendly or acquainted with is structured by geographical proximity (living in the same community) and institutional member-ship and organization (attending the same (pre)school, and being in the same stream or set), both of which condition motility and the likelihood of time-space path convergence – the one-off or repeated encounters in which friends are first met – and both of which are already conditioned heavily by possession of economic and cultural capital (McPherson et al., 2001). Moreover, when it comes to very young chil-dren there is evidence that 'friends', or routine playmates, are selected and filtered according to parental taste – whether the playmate's parents are 'like us', 'respectable' and so on (Howes, 1998). When children are a little older, and forming connections with others themselves, then the principle of homophily kicks in, initially intuited not by a full sense of one's place in the social space, which is still only emerging, but *according to difference from the dispositions and doxic schemes of perception forged in one's family field*. Research directly on class in this regard is actually relatively rare, though it is noticeable in the most famous studies of school-ing, from Willis (1977) and Mac an Ghaill (1994) to Reay et al. (2011), that 'birds of a feather flock together' as the cliché goes. Moreover, studies specifically on the formation of friendships in early life have noted that children tend to gravitate towards one another on the basis of common dis-positions for certain styles of play – whether imaginative or 'rough and tumble', for example – shared (dis)taste for 'anti-social behaviour' (by which they mean fighting, resisting teachers, bullying others) – and parity of level of scholastic 'achievement' (Tuma and Hallinan, 1979; Rubin et al., 1994; Hartup, 1998). All of these can, perhaps, be taken as rough proxies for relative possession of and orientation towards practical mastery/physical capital or symbolic mastery/cultural capital. Sales' (2012) ethnography of primary school children in a disadvantaged community, however, provides more direct evidence that children as young as five tend to come together on the basis of similarity – and denigrate those deemed different – according to not just class (as mediated by family doxa) but class fraction too. Corsaro (2015) also makes clear that with time, as children move into adolescence, friendship networks and peer groups become much more heavily stratified and exclusive on the basis of a variety of capitals.

Yet none of this takes away from the fact that those social networks have, in return, their own effect on the habitus and even, as social capital (likely to become decreasingly volatile over time), objective positioning – something recognized by Bourdieu and Passeron (1990: 157), but only hastily. Like time-space location, routinized contacts may specify wider perception of social similarity and difference by providing concrete models or 'prototypes' of sections of social space, displaying particular symbols and acting in particular ways, which will forever inform perception and evaluation of anonymous or experientially distant others. Moreover, homophily is only ever rough and ready, with networks still bringing together individuals with at least micro-differences in capitals and ethos as well as unique family spirits, and specified by local context. As Sales (2012) found, two children otherwise hailing from families far apart within the dominant class may pair up and influence one another's views, tastes and possibilities when their lifeworlds are situated in an environment (neighbourhood, school, etc.) disproportionately populated by the dominated, but they may have had nothing to do with one another, and been on opposing sides of localized symbolic struggle (with its lasting effects on habitus), in an environment dominated by the dominant.

Finally, both networks and the experience of time-space, and with them the integration into social space, are further structured by the operation and interaction of several microfields into which the child is simultaneously incorporated – or, in short, by proliferating *multiplicity*, transformation of single-field habitus into a multifaceted *social surface* and differentiation of the *world horizon*. The idea that neighbourhoods can, in certain circumstances, be conceived as local social spaces offering alternative modes of misrecognition for those debarred from the capitals legitimated by the education system, and generating distinct struggles and symbolic boundaries, has already been broached and will be taken up again in the next chapter (see also Atkinson, 2015a, 2015b; in relation to young people specifically see Sales, 2012). That schools too, as nodes within the wider space of educational establishments, may constitute small-scale fields (rather than 'total institutions' or 'institutional habitus') with their own effects on pupils' experience has also been explored before (Atkinson, 2011a). Both, which often go under the labels of 'neighbourhood effects' and 'school effects' in existing educational research, but also the perceptual embedding of the family spirit in a wider system of difference and symbolic domination, can have effects, in turn, on the familial field, nourishing tension, conflict, alternative models to identify with, heterodox aspirations and subversion – a desire to 'escape' into another class world, for example, or to be like a media figure or 'local legend' – depending on the state of play in the field of familial forces and distance between objective possibilities in the national and local social space and institutionally lauded futures (see e.g. Ingram, 2011). Indeed, as in adult life, this multiplicity is the source of what might be described as the real source of 'double (or multiple) binds': we desire and are pressured to find worth and recognition in many fields at once when ascent in one may, in fact, necessitate sacrifice of capital accumulation – with all the suffering that entails – in another.

What stands for integration into the social space and symbolic space – the social structures I have studied closest – stands, I would conjecture, for implication into the national ethno-racial space: the increasing situation of parental desires and doxa within a larger space of struggle via media, schooling, locale and friendships clusters, and the tensions and conflicts it can produce, run along parallel lines. Gender too is fundamental to the process of social becoming, but it has been somewhat bracketed in the foregoing because, being so important yet working in a slightly different way to both class and ethno-racial domination (something Bourdieu did not articulate clearly enough), it deserves separate attention. Before we can make sense of its reproduction, its place in family struggles and its interrelation with the social space, in other words, we first need to do a little conceptual ground clearing.

5

Gender

Strong on class, weak on gender – that seems to have been the general assessment of Bourdieu's corpus amongst feminists. Adkins and Skeggs' (2004) landmark volume of engagements with the French thinker is perhaps the clearest articulation of this sentiment, but it is obvious enough from the last few decades of scholarship that, on the one hand, Bourdieu's reworking of class in terms of habitus, capital and social space has provided fruitful tools for bringing that once unfashionable concept back into feminist thought, yet that, on the other, his own musings on gender in *Masculine Domination* (Bourdieu, 2001) have hardly won legions of feminist fans. Feminists have chosen, instead, to innovate when thinking about how class and gender interact, to turn to alternative streams of thought in gender studies and to conclude as a result that Bourdieu's toolkit should be pillaged and remoulded rather than adopted wholesale. A whole array of new quasi-Bourdieusian concepts have sprung up in the process, from 'gender capital' (Skeggs, 2004; Huppatz, 2009; cf. Miller, 2014) and 'erotic capital' (Hakim, 2012) to the 'field of gender' (Coles, 2007).

Why precisely have Bourdieu's writings on gender and its relationship to other forms of domination been deemed so bad? There seem to be several core arguments, their key articulators being, among others, Armengaud et al. (1995), Lovell (2000), Anthias (2001), Mottier (2002), Connolly (2004), Skeggs (2004), Witz (2004), Silva (2005) and Connell (2007). First of all, the critics claim, he deploys a rigid binary model that homogenizes the experiences of men and women, partly because of an unjustified universalization from his favoured empirical example: the Berbers of Kabylia in the mid-twentieth century. He thus not only overlooks the contemporary complexity of gender differences (androgyny, third genders, transsexualism, etc.) but sees women as uniformly dominated and cannot grasp either resistance and struggle or the fact that femininity may act as a resource in some situations. Secondly, he fails to engage in any significant way with feminist literature and, as a result, ends up making outdated or unsophisticated arguments. Finally, he prioritizes class to the extent of refusing to see gender as a structuring factor in social space.

In all cases the premise is sound enough: because of his interest in substantive questions and his distaste for scholastic theoreticism, Bourdieu *did* rely heavily on his old Kabyle research to reveal the general features of gender division, ancient and contemporary, in his book on the topic, he *did* shy away from out-and-out confrontation with the leading figures of feminist theory (though in fairness he did draw on a decent amount of relevant research) and he *was* brief, and a little vague, on the relationship between gender, class and other social struggles. But there is no need to throw the baby out with the bathwater. If we gather up some of Bourdieu's thoughts and findings on gender, if we clarify and elaborate on his concise statements, if we draw comparisons with compatible strands of thought in feminism and gender studies to bulk them out, and, crucially, if we push in the direction of relational phenomenology – as interested in the relationships between fields in individual life-worlds as in fields themselves – we see that, in actuality, a perspective faithful to the logical hard core of Bourdieu's approach, suitably nuanced, provides plenty of strong tools for coherently conceptualizing and researching masculine domination. They might even harmonize with many of the advances of contemporary feminist theory while managing to avoid its imbalances and confused concepts.

To put my reading of Bourdieu in a nutshell, gender is not a capital or field itself but a mode of classifying the world which has been historically entwined with the monopolization of certain forms of (mis)recognition, or capitals, across *multiple* fields such that those forms of (mis)recognition have come to be seen as inherently, or at least overwhelmingly, masculine or feminine.[1] An androcentric social order is, therefore, one in which men have managed to disproportionately accumulate certain valued properties across different fields – 'strength', 'rationality', 'drive', 'intelligence', etc. – to such a degree that masculinity is equated in perception with those valued properties. At the same time, of course, this means that many relatively autonomous social divisions and modes of domination are perceived in the everyday lifeworld as facets of gender difference.

This reading will be developed in a number of steps. First, what exactly gender is will be clarified, leading into a discussion of its association with particular capitals and a reflection on the relationship between social construction and biology. The chapter then sketches the historical sociogenesis of masculine domination and its maintenance before considering the nexus of gender and class today and then, finally, the experience of gender in the everyday lifeworld. In each case the task will be to try to elucidate Bourdieu's own position, answer critics by clearing up misconceptions, compare it with other strands of thought and bulk it up by making suitable – that is, coherent and consistent – additions. Along the way it will be seen that some of the Bourdieu-inspired concepts developed by feminists and others are rather more problematic than their frequent use would suggest.

A scheme of perception

Like anything, gender is, for Bourdieu, both a *relational* matter and, ultimately, bound up with struggles for *recogni-*

tion, but in a very particular way. It is, at root, a mode of categorizing the world oriented around the binary opposition of 'male' and 'female', or 'masculinity' and 'femininity', in which each category derives its meaning and properties from the other (to be a 'man' is to not act 'like a woman' and vice versa). This is a source of consternation for those detractors levelling charges of over-simplicity and homogenization at Bourdieu (esp. McCall, 1992; Mottier, 2002; Witz, 2004), but the allegations seem to confuse Bourdieu's usual *empirical example* – the Berbers of Kabylia, for whom it seems, in the absence of appropriate empirical counter-examples, that the gender binary was clear and rigid there at the time of his research – with the *conceptual principle*. They thus unduly generalize from the former to the latter when in fact the general principle of opposition is much suppler than supposed.

To begin with, consider what are actually said to be opposed: not eternal essences or neatly bounded groups, but linguistic-perceptual *constructions*, i.e. categories of thought associated with certain practices, symbols and signs which have become more or less doxic. They are analogous to Connell's (2005) conception of 'hegemonic masculinity' and 'emphasized femininity' – cultural ideals as to what men and women should be – insofar as *people approximate them to greater or lesser degrees* in practice and, in fact, are measured against them as more or less 'manly', a 'sissy', 'butch', 'girly', etc. Hence Bourdieu's assertion that men are dominated by masculine domination too: there is a constant pressure to 'live up to' the idealized doxic category (Bourdieu, 2001: 69; Bourdieu and Wacquant, 1992: 173). On seeing or meeting another person, therefore, people not only, as the ethnomethodologists Kessler and McKenna (1978) astutely analysed, automatically attribute one of the two gender categories to them on the basis of the interpretation of the full gamut of symbols (body shape, clothing, hair, etc.) and behaviours (vocal tone, mannerisms, gait, tastes, specific practices) associated with them, never mind the signs that might be used to denote them ('look at *him*', 'here's

Will'). At the same time they pre-predicatively perceive on the basis of the precise combination of symbols the *extent* to which they resemble the cardinal categories ('he's an effeminate man', 'she's a butch woman'), with all the typified valuations and expectations that go along with that, including the degree to which the person perceived is seen as 'like me' or 'unlike me' in their position between the two poles.

Sometimes, of course, the precise blend of symbols (and signs) can confound one's schemes of perception and bring the usually automatic gender attribution process to consciousness ('is that a man or a woman?'), as in Diane Margolis' run-in with an androgynous shop assistant cited by West and Zimmerman (1987: 133–4). Moreover, the principle of opposition does not preclude the development of an abundance of more refined classifications and signs denoting the space *between* the two opposites and deriving their sense thus, that is, in precisely the same way as 'the petite bourgeoisie' does through its position between the dominant and dominated in social space (this is recognized by Moi, 1991). From homosexuality and effeminacy to androgyny and transsexualism, all are categorizations of specific mixtures and weightings of modes of behaviour and symbolism associated with the two poles in different cultures. The resulting system of embodied and objectified constructions, furnishing an expanded range of thinkable and possible actions in how to 'act like a man/woman', might not look all that different from Connell's (2005) model of the 'gender order' splitting the masculine pole into hegemonic (firmly heterosexual, strong, etc.), subordinated (effeminate, homosexual), complicit (struggling with varying success to be hegemonic) and marginal (overly violent, macho, etc.) varieties and the feminine pole into emphasized (compliant, caring, etc.) and resistant ('butch', lesbian, feminist) forms, all still defined in fully relational terms (as for Connell) through their relative mix of symbols and behaviours from the two extremes.

The question of biology

The notion that gender is a changeable, relational mode of classifying the world inevitably raises the question of how that classification system relates to the seeming constant of human biology. If we are to believe Silva (2005), who otherwise curiously claims not to be describing him as a biological determinist (p. 93), the foundations of the gender binary for Bourdieu lie in biological differences 'standing outside history and culture' (p. 91). He assumes, she says, a 'determining link between biology and culture', sees sexed identity or the sexed body as 'given' and universal (p. 92), is thus unable to see how there could be deviation from 'generalizations' and ignores historical research – specifically that of Thomas Laqueur (1990) – demonstrating that the scientific construction of sexual categories is in fact a 'cultural project' (Silva, 2005: 93). In reality, however, Bourdieu's (2001) argument is rather more subtle than that. Without lapsing into an outright idealism, he contends that there is a circular (p. 11) but – compared to essentialism – *inverted* (p. 22) relationship of causation between anatomy and the socially constituted opposition of 'male' and 'female'. Typically he conveys this with catchy, though potentially misleading, phrases like 'the socialization of the biological and the biologicization of the social' (p. 3), but he is otherwise quite clear on this.

Anatomy, he argues, *appears* to be the natural justification of the division between male and female, it *appears* to furnish an 'essence' to gender which *appears* to give it an air of eternity, yet this is, in fact, nothing more than the historical product of a long labour of social construction. Of course there are certain physiological realities (or 'matrices of universals' as Bourdieu calls them) which mean that constructions of gender are not *completely* 'undetermined' (p. 11) – someone with an XX chromosomal makeup, for example, cannot give birth.[2] But the perception of sexual anatomy or physiology as radically distinct – the 'social definition of the sex organs', sexual activity or the body, and by extension gender *per se*, in terms of oppositions (in/out, hard/soft, active/passive, male/female, etc.) – is no 'simple recording of natural properties, directly offered to perception' but the artefact of a *categorization of an uncategorized reality* involving 'an accentuation of certain differences and the scotomization of [i.e. blindness to] certain similarities' (p. 14). Other figures in gender studies, as it happens, use almost exactly the same language to make the same point. For example, Laqueur (1990: 19) – who Bourdieu (2001: 15), contrary to Silva's (2005) claims, happily cites – notes in his history of scientific constructions of sex that 'humans impose their sense of opposition onto a world of continuous shades of difference and similarity', whilst Connell (1987: 80), in her effort to surmount the opposition between idealism and biological reductionism, argues that, rather than reflecting natural processes, human practice involves 'weaving a structure of symbol and interpretation around them, and often vastly exaggerating or distorting them', with the 'social emphasis on difference negat[ing] natural similarity' and internal heterogeneity through multiple 'denials, transformations and contradictions' (cf. also Rubin, 1975).

In other words, then, though there may be tendencies and generalities of chromosomes and hormones shaping physique and reproductive capacities, the sheer *variety* and *complexity* of biological processes (including not just scientifically constructed categories like intersexuality and pseudohermaphroditism but also the great range of variation within the two polar constructions), plus their lack of direct impact on, and indeed possible manipulation by, human action, mean that nothing – from voice or body shape to genital anatomy – acts as an inherent foundation for the splitting of gender (or sex) into two bounded categories. This is instead a *pre-existing* construction of the world through which physiology is interpreted and articulated – including by scientists (cf. Kessler and McKenna, 1978). As Bourdieu (2001: 3n.3) notes critically of contemporary psychological research, for example, it 'takes over the common vision of the sexes as radically separate sets, without intersections', from everyday practice and 'ignores the degree of *overlap* between the distributions of male and female performances and the differences (of magnitude) between the differences observed in various domains (from sexual anatomy to intelligence).' Yet at the same time, being invested with immense symbolic power, psychology and other sciences legitimate the everyday binary perception they import by feeding it back to the populace with the authoritative stamp of scientific truth.

Symbolic struggle and gendered dispositions

Science is not, however, all of a piece, either between or within disciplines, but a cluster of fields in which people struggle to assert the legitimate definition of the truth (Bourdieu, 2004a). The precise construction of gender and sex perpetuated by specific individuals within those fields will, therefore, bear the trace of that struggle insofar as there will be dominant and dominated visions defined against one another and greater or lesser degrees of contestation. Not only that, but the scientific constructions of gender and sex align, merge and compete with the constructions of gender and sex emanating from struggles going on in other fields – the religious field, the legal field, the media field, the artistic field, the political and bureaucratic fields and so on. If there is a common scheme of perception defining the symbols, practices and values that are and should be associated with masculinity and femininity, in other words, and if there are changes, elaborations and refinements of this scheme over time to complicate, revise or bolster the traditional binary, then both have to be rooted within the machinations of *the field of power* – to be more precise, national fields of power, but also, increasingly, the international field of power, or world-regional fields of power, with some capacity to decree what must be dealt with within national fields of power. This is a mechanism often missing in feminist writing. Connell (2005), for example, recognizes that the categories of the gender order are the product of power and a 'political process', but lacks the concrete means for conceptualizing the clash of interests and differentials of symbolic power underpinning them.

In fact, just as it does in relation to the notion of 'family', the field of power plays a dual role. On the one hand it is the arena where dominant and alternative conceptions of gender – what men and women are and should be in biological, behavioural or moral terms – are established, struggled over and challenged in line with different interests. In order to halt their decline in the social space by clinging on to what means of power and privilege they have, for example, the petite bourgeoisie's representatives in the political field tend to champion a somewhat conservative view of gender relations, while certain sections of the intellectual field, as a means of challenging a social order which currently confines them to a dominated position within the field of power, seek to subvert the status quo in relation to gender relations as much as anything else. Often, of course, these struggles are fed by the experiences and privations articulated by movements, collectives or individuals outside the field of power proper – artists, politicians, intellectuals and media outlets may embrace them, and seek to give them a 'voice', in their own struggle for recognition. In contemporary Western societies, for example, the advance of feminism and the gay movement – with their numerous representatives and sympathizers within national fields of power – have been instrumental in turning the previously rigid set of gender categories from unquestioned doxa into an *orthodoxy* counterposed to a *heterodoxy* proclaiming alternative visions of capacities and meanings, opening gender out into the variety of expressions and categories described earlier, though some underpinning assumptions around gender and sex doubtless remain doxic nonetheless.

On the other hand, the agents within the field of power, thanks to their symbolic capital, possess the capacity to deliver the gendered doxa, orthodoxy and heterodoxy forged in their struggles through time-space into the lifeworlds of the population at large within a given social order, even beyond it, via interweaving circuits of symbolic power. The media and journalistic fields, with their alliances and homologies with other fields, play a disproportionate role in this process, transmitting and often 'interpreting' (i.e. glossing with their own schemes of evaluation) the assumptions encoded in political speeches, religious decrees and cultural products (including films and television programmes), but so too does the chain of associations between people and things cutting across myriad fields constituting schooling. Through the injunctions (e.g. 'big boys don't cry', 'take it like a man') and expectations of what is 'normal' or 'to be done' by members of each gender (e.g. girls play with dolls and wear dresses) they continuously bring into everyday situations and encounters from a tender age (see e.g. Lloyd, 1987), they contribute to the process whereby gender categories are, ultimately, *made flesh* in dispositions towards one's body – how one should look and carry oneself – and in attitudes and anticipations, producing a gait, a bearing, an appearance, capacities, skills, desires, perceptions, self-perceptions, discourses and tastes and thus a set of more or less integrated actions and behaviours. Rounding out the relationship between perception and physiology, the categories of thought are incorporated and shape biological appearance (through, for example, diet, physical activity, body modification), thus giving the *impression* that biology is the cause rather than the effect of binary differences (Vandebroeck, forthcoming). In short, 'the social principle of division constructs the anatomical difference' which then, through its embodiment in durable dispositions, 'becomes the basis and apparently natural justification of the social vision which founds it' (Bourdieu, 2001: 11).

Two caveats need to be made here to clear up some reservations. First of all, dispositions being gendered does not mean, as Silva (2005: 96) and others claim, that there is no more or less conscious *manipulation* of gendered symbols in order to influence self-presentation. Just as a class habitus can give rise to strategies of self-presentation, so gendered dispositions can spawn strategies aiming to attain desired outcomes in different situations – for example, emphasizing particular features typified with masculinity or femininity to attract a partner, or hiding certain behaviours or features for work purposes – it being understood that there is a set of durable, sedimented attitudes which generate the motivation for and probability and likely character of such strategies. Here lies one of the major differences with Judith Butler, the feminist theorist whose work has been compared and contrasted with Bourdieu's approach quite enough (see e.g. McNay, 1999; Lovell, 2000; Fowler, 2003), though perhaps the most sociologically pertinent advance over Butler's stance is that a Bourdieusian perspective provides concepts and tools for unravelling how the continuously 'performed' gender 'ideals' (or doxa) that Butler talks about are socially generated, disseminated and incorporated, namely, the field of power and circuits of symbolic power – all of which remain rather vague in Butler's analysis.

Secondly, the genesis of gendered dispositions is by no means, as some critics have asserted, necessarily a case of smooth reproduction and unquestioned conformity to one of the two ideal-typical poles according to Bourdieu, of *a priori* rejection of resistance, struggle and complexity (Lovell, 2004), even if, admittedly, Bourdieu himself hardly explored this point. In reality the reception of gendered ideals emanating from the field of power will be filtered, not only by one's place in the time-space circuits of symbolic power – differentiating, for example, rural and urban experiences, or regional experiences, but also experiences in particular schools, neighbourhoods and so on – but by the positions occupied in multiple spaces of struggle by oneself *and* one's significant others. How they are read, evaluated and assimilated, and the thinkable and unthinkable practices, projects and self-attributions (or subjective 'field of possibles') they foster, will differ according to one's schemes of perception in relation to, and the balance of one's libido across, a multitude of fields, some large, some small. These include class, large-scale fields of production and organizational fields (workplaces, institutions, etc.), but none is as important, since it is the microcosm in which childhood dispositions and desires are primarily forged, as the family field, with its alliances and rifts, tensions and pleasures, models and anti-models, identifications and rejections in the struggle for affective recognition. Connell's (2005) dissection of the reactions and typifications and the escalating schisms and shifting coalitions within families – conceived, in her own words, as a 'field of relationships' (p. 146) – following perceived infractions and behaviours of the child in matters of gender and sexuality can be fruitfully reconceived thus, for example, as a means of grasping elements of the social genesis of the subjective field of possibles – a phrase Connell herself uses (p. 149) – regarding gender and sexuality. The key point, however, is that individual gendered dispositions, their degree of similarity and difference from those of others and their degree of conformity and resistance to prevailing orthodoxy, are forged in the lifeworld according to the individual's specific location in numerous circuits and fields. For that reason, it is more precise to conceive of gendered dispositions not just in terms of habitus, in relation to a single field, but as a phenomenon of one's *social surface*.

From gender capital to gendered capitals

The implication of the foregoing argument is that gender does not, contrary to Coles' (2007) bold assertion, form a field unto itself. Indeed, Coles' theorization of gender as a field lapses into some of the errors already encountered, since in claiming that the field of gender is actually composed of two sub-fields, one for masculinity and one for femininity, he reinstates the kind of rigid binary dismissed earlier as it becomes difficult to plot and make sense of the transgendered at all (are they in neither sub-field or both?). At the same time, by admitting that the sub-field of masculinity is largely structured by economic, cultural and social capital – i.e. class resources – as well as ethnicity (which is a field of its own), age and sexuality, he undercuts any claim to its relative autonomy. Nor is it particularly logical or fruitful to speak of a 'gender capital', whether defined in terms of hege-monic masculinity or emphasized femininity, within the social space or other fields, for that is to obscure the *multitude* of principles of misrecognition and power acting as the sources of androcentrism, and feminine resistance or 'niches', across *multiple* fields. It is, instead, to take masculine domination as given, failing to unpick the threads of its genesis and venturing into tautology (men are dominant because they are men), as well as to unhelpfully reduce its myriad components and their varying interrelations in individual lives to a single dimension – one might even say, to a substance.

However, while it may not be reducible to a single capital, the system of constructions of gender is closely entwined with relative possession of two forms of power, authority and (mis)recognition – in other words capital – operating specifically through bodily capacity and appearance. Coles refers to the first of these, *physical* capital, but like Shilling (2003), on whom he draws, he seems to reduce this down to class dispositions and age from the start, arguing that young and dominant class bodies have more physical capital. More fruitfully, following Bourdieu (1990b: 122; cf. Wacquant, 1995, 2004), physical capital should be conceived as the capital of *fighting strength, physical force, and martial skill* – i.e. perceived corporeal capacity to subjugate or dominate directly, including sexually, whether by hand or (its objectified form) weapon. Secondly, there is the capital briefly alluded to by Bourdieu (1984: 202–8), albeit in a way which left its conceptual status decidedly unclear (cf. also Skeggs, 1997: 128; Wacquant, 2004: 220–5), and taken up more wholeheartedly in recent times by others keen to stress its contemporary significance (e.g. Martin and George, 2006): 'erotic' or 'sexual' capital. Intimately linked to the specifically sexualized libido, seduction and fantasy, this consists of misrecognition flowing from possession of a combination of features which are defined and experienced as 'attractive', a 'turn on' and so on in a particular social order. Polarized by gender, there are orthodox and heterodox definitions, of course, dominant and dominated, conservative and subversive positions in the struggle to define and embody sexual attractiveness and virility and thus a distinct space of possibles. There is also an autonomous pole of the field, where desirability and (self-)worth are defined purely in terms of certain characteristics of physiognomy, anatomy, posture and adornment as well as known or assumed sexual prowess, and a heteronomous pole, where outside principles, including economic capital, cultural capital or even physical capital, influence perception of someone's sexual appeal. Like physical capital, the more autonomous version of sexual capital, while to some degree bounded by the potentialities of the body given at birth, can be developed and accumulated through investment of other resources (in gym memberships, surgery, attire, etc.), but the latter is hardly necessary.

This rendering of sexual capital, however, has to be distinguished from those offered by many of the concept's most ardent advocates since, to be blunt, they tend to be fairly poorly constructed. Hakim (2012), for example, in line with her previous post-feminist 'preference theory' of female labour market participation, anchors it (and cultural capital) in a largely individualist, asocial, free-choosing conception of human beings in which the cultivation of capital at the expense of others is vaunted as a way for women to 'get ahead'. She thus misses the fact that it is, in fact, a *principle of double domination* – on the one hand, of those deemed 'ugly', and, on the other, of even the apparently dominant since, like Beauvoir's (2010) hetaeras, women rich in this capital are chasing forms of recognition defined largely by men's desires. Green's (2008, 2014) work on sexual capital avoids some of these problems, but his tendency to focus on thousands of tiny and fairly isolated 'sexual fields' comprised of localized interactional networks (or what he calls 'circuits') of individuals focused on particular bars, clubs, websites and so on, is unconvincing, as this rather obscures that the genesis and value of the properties and desires plied within those sites – all better described as specific *market places* – are ultimately determined by a wider (national and increasingly international) space of difference influenced significantly by the ideas of those within the field of power (not least the media field). The desires and properties of particular categories of homosexual, such as 'bears' or 'leathermen', only make sense when put in relation to all other desires and properties vis-à-vis sexuality – their opposition, subversion, subordination and so on. He also seems to view it primarily in terms of a struggle for partners and obscures the allied struggle to impose certain properties as 'attractive' and, thus, be misrecognized as such. Illouz (2012) offers an advance in this respect with her own notion of the sexual field, seeing it as a broad-scale arena of recognition and misrecognition struggles, but she appears to conflate struggles to impose and embody ideals of attractiveness and virility with the quest for love, ascribing the former to the masculine libido and the latter to women. Although they doubtless interact, it seems analytically sharper to distinguish the field of struggle over sexual attractiveness and prowess from the micro-field in which love as a form of capital is sought and won, namely, the family, even if sexual capital (like physical capital) can become a heteronomous principle of power in the latter.

In any case, while possession of and struggles over physical and sexual capital – in neighbourhood social spaces, family fields, specific fields (sports, modelling, etc.) or markets where schemes of perception recognize them as legitimate – differentiate perception and give substantive character to perceptions of masculinity and femininity, they are neither reducible nor intrinsic to being socially categorized as 'male' or 'female'. Moreover, the everyday concepts of 'man' and 'woman', and the associations and expectations that go with them (what men and women can, will and should do) are tied up to different degrees with other forms of capital, and the symbols and *illusio* paired with them, too – cultural capital and economic capital, for instance, or familial symbolic capital. A man deemed 'unattractive' or 'weak' is still perceived as a 'man' on the basis of certain properties, therefore, and possesses other advantages of

capital accumulation. Historically, however, those categorized as 'men' have tended to monopolize physical force such
that it has become more closely associated in perception with
the masculine pole and, in particular, with hegemonic forms
of masculinity, leaving 'women' with particular forms
of sexual capital as a primary source of bodily capital. So
while both masculinity and femininity *appear* to operate as
resources this is, in fact, nothing more than an illusion –
there is no 'gender capital' in general, or a 'gender field', but
particular gender*ed* capitals being mobilized in specific
structural contexts.

Perhaps the underpinning contrast is with Beauvoir's
(2010) famous existentialist-phenomenological conception
of gender. She too conceived it as oriented around a perceptual binary, and she too located it within struggles for recognition and justification. Her starting point, however, was
Hegel, as notoriously read by Kojève (1969), and his conception of the struggle for recognition in terms of the Master–
Slave dialectic: two parties engage in an initial struggle, but
one, fearing death, relents, recognizing and thus serving the
other as Master, while the Master goes on to dominate,
though inherently undermined by the fact that they do not
recognize their new Slave as someone from whom recognition is valued (they are seen as 'inessential'). Eventually, the
Slave, having worked on nature in the meantime for the
Master and mastered the art of changing and developing
the world ('transcendence'), and knowing that the current
state of recognition does not exhaust all possibilities, will
take up the fight again, overturn the current state of relations
and resolve the dialectic. The blueprint for the Marxist conception of class lies herein, of course, but Beauvoir applies
it to gender by declaring men to be the Master (or the
Subject) and women to be the Slave (or the Other) throughout history, though with the added twists that (i) this is
because men have been seen as masters of transcendence and
(ii) because women do not form a homogeneous group like
the proletariat, they have not been able to meaningfully
battle back – they are always the losers in the struggle for

recognition, in other words. Some may interpret this – since capital is by definition a source of (mis)recognition – as grounds for saying that being a man constitutes a symbolic capital of some sort. But the view here (I do not claim it was Bourdieu's view) is different. The principle of recognition is not being a man or a woman *per se*, but the properties each category tends to possess (e.g. physical or cultural capital), and, while men and women can both possess these properties to different degrees, since those defined as 'men' have managed to secure a quasi-monopoly on certain valued properties, two processes ensure masculinity is equated in perception with dominant forms of domination. The first of these is *allodoxia*, in which men are seen in general as strong, intelligent (or 'rational'), driven, rightful leaders and so on, and thus superior by association, even when specific individuals are poorly endowed with the capital underpinning those associations. The second is *sociodicy*, as those who possess capital believe and foster the belief that it derives from innate capacities – and that if others do or want to display the associated behaviours or practices it is 'unnatural' – in order to justify and maintain their position of power. Ultimately, recognition is never a binary of recognized–unrecognized, as in Hegel's (or Kojève's) eminently *scholastic* vision of two abstract individuals or homogeneous groups engaged in isolated struggle outside concrete history, but a case of being misrecognized to different degrees in relation to multiple specific sources of potential misrecognition.

His/Herstory

Let us now put some flesh on these bones by delving a little into the historical genesis of gender categories, their transformation over time and how they have come to be paired with particular sources of misrecognition and symbolic power. Bourdieu's own view on this is largely implicit and under-discussed, but it begins with the Berbers of Kabylia, not simply because they are an example of a pre-industrial, pre-capitalist, undifferentiated society, but because they were (at least in the 1950s, when Bourdieu was in the field) nothing less than an 'anthropological sanctuary' retaining to a high degree of 'practical coherence and integrity' the 'ancient Mediterranean traditions' which, being shared by the oft-studied ancient Greeks, laid the foundations for European culture in general (Bourdieu, 1997b: 192; 2001: 6–7). In fact, in one place, though without much evidence, Bourdieu (2005b: 46) rather boldly suggested that the orientation found here has persisted since Neolithic times.

These claims for Kabylia's special status are, to be sure, overblown, not least because Bourdieu never mentions the likely influence of Islam on the Berbers (see Lane, 2000; Goodman and Silverstein, 2009). That aside, in this particular social order gender was, argued Bourdieu (2001: 10), construed as a rigid binary and, furthermore, inserted within a whole cosmology of homologous oppositions – hard/soft, high/low, inside/outside, dry/wet, etc. – organizing perception and action. This applied to language, clothing, gait, the body, temporal divisions, uses of space – from within the famous Kabyle house to the split between public and private space – and divisions of labour, such as men carrying out the quick and violent act of slaughtering a pig while the women conduct the long and slow process of preparing its meat. Finding their 'natural confirmation' (i.e. legitimation) in 'geographical oppositions, biological cycles, agrarian or cosmic cycles' (Bourdieu, 1997b: 194), this system of oppositions valorized and, therefore, accorded symbolic power (or honour), to those poles of the binaries associated with masculinity, making it 'phallonarcissistic' or 'androcentric' in character, and is rationalized and justified in all manner of creation myths, or cosmogonies, serving as a sociodicy of male privilege (Bourdieu, 2001: 18–19).

The true origins of the supremacy accorded to masculinity, however, is said to be rooted in 'the logic of the economy of symbolic exchange', i.e. the fact that women function as *objects of exchange* in the matrimonial market, traded by men (the *subjects* of the exchange) to maximize familial and, ultimately, male symbolic and material power (Bourdieu and Wacquant, 1992: 173–4; Bourdieu, 2001: 42–9). This in turn – following Lévi-Strauss (1969), it seems – is founded on the incest taboo, which apparently 'entails the necessity of exchange as equal communication amongst men' (Bourdieu, 2001: 43). Here we have, to my mind, the weakest part of Bourdieu's work on gender insofar as it seems to lapse into some of the errors and crudities we have already tried to stay clear of: it is disappointingly tautological (men are dominant because they use women to maintain their dominance), reminiscent of Beauvoir's unsatisfactory Subject/Other split, and unable to explain the variety of gendered roles and rankings across historical and contemporary cultures. We need, therefore, to retrace the story, at least in broad brushstrokes.

There is no reason to disagree with Beauvoir's (2010) own starting point: in the earliest hunter-gather societies, some individuals continuously bore and reared children and others did not, the former tending to be less able as a result to engage in hunting practices. We can underscore, with the weight of contemporary archaeological evidence, that this represents a *practical adaptation* rather than an expression of *essence*, since potential/actual childbearers can and did/do successfully engage in hunting practices where particular conditions allow or necessitate it (Kuhn and Stiner, 2006). Yet around this basic difference, specified by local conditions and adjustments, wove a polarizing practical scheme of perception emphasizing difference, drawing associations and homologies and hiding similarities in the way described above. We can depart, moreover, from Beauvoir's philosophical inference: it was not 'man's' perceived capacity for transcendence (transformation of nature and innovation), opposed to 'women's' supposed 'immanence' (the association of reproduction with repetition and stasis), that really mattered. Rather – and this is no more than a hypothesis – it was strategies to impose the physical capacities (skills, strength) and orientations (bravery) cultivated in the practice of hunting and its human-focused training grounds (e.g. wrestling) – i.e. forms of physical capital – as symbolic capital within the local social space, to pair this with other symbols and signs usually co-given with it to construct folk notions of 'masculinity' as opposed to 'femininity' and to work to monopolize it with greater or lesser success. Gender is, in other words, a primordial case of 'group making' and closure. This would really have kicked off around the same time as *homo sapiens* flourished in its use of language and symbolism, in the Upper Palaeolithic era, eventually giving rise to the Dumezilean triangle, in which possessors of physical capital (warriors) are more or less opposed to possessors of the capital of control over symbolic/sign systems conceiving humanity's place in the cosmos (shamans, seers, spiritualists, etc.), and both of these are opposed to those excluded from these powers. Since men disproportionately (but not automatically or totally) had the conditions of existence allowing access to both of these capitals, i.e. freedom from childbearing and rearing, they could monopolize both forms of power and, even if they were antagonistic between themselves, use them to perpetuate the androcentric sociodicy that their power derives from natural or divine constitution. The advent of agriculture and more complex social orders, from ancient Mesopotamia to classical Greece, can be seen as elaborations of regional social spaces with extended time-space circuits of symbolic power built on these principles of opposition.

So how did we get from there to contemporary capitalist Western societies where the androcentric worldview persists and is maintained by the family and the field of power (Bourdieu, 2001: 85ff), even if the rise of feminization, feminism and the gay movement has refracted the original binary into the more complex system of hegemonic orthodoxies and dominated heterodoxies mentioned earlier? Bourdieu himself is not much help here (see Lane, 2006), but it can be inferred that the relative monopoly of the physical capital of force and the capital of mastery of symbolic/sign systems – as the incipient form of religious capital and then, later, cultural capital – were codified and legitimated in a succession of sociodicies. Most significant was the Judeo-Christian cosmology which spread throughout Roman and feudal Europe and, in turn, underlay the early scientific vision of gender in terms of possession of different permutations of the same anatomy, one inferior, one superior, in line with the 'great chain of being' (Laqueur, 1990). The latter was later overhauled by the rationalist rupture of the Enlightenment and pitted *against* religion within so many regional fields of power, though it was still undertaken by, and thus laden with the perceptions of, men. In any case, both religion and science were fundamental to the vision perpetuated and enforced by states, or the emergent bureaucratic fields, given the evolving structures of the overall fields of power (Bourdieu, 2014; on family policy, see, e.g., Lenoir, 2003). This fed into not only the evolution of male-centred economic fields through industrialization – with the bourgeois construction of the breadwinner/homemaker family as a sign of 'success', and with that the channelling of women's libidos primarily towards the family field, eventually trickling down the social space (see Fowler, 2003) – but also, as Connell (2005) has rightly noted, the global exportation and imposition of European schemata of perception through imperialism.

At the same time, as Elias (2000) has done most to demonstrate, there was a fundamental shift in the legitimate definition of masculinity and its relation to physical capital. Physical capital, the capacity to use violence or threat of violence to secure recognition and advantage, was still, along with the capital deriving from religious authority in the form of assertions of divine heritage, a key principle of difference and domination in post-Roman Europe, with warlords converting it into economic capital and (with the display of the items, such as jewellery, it afforded) symbolic capital via the extraction of surplus ('tribute') from agrarian client populations (on Anglo-Saxon England, for example, see Bassett, 1989; Yorke, 1990; for its development with feudalization, see Mann, 1986). Over time, with the emergence of court societies and domination through the symbolic capital of honour and 'good behaviour', i.e. through symbolic violence, physical violence and its associated capital were not only slowly replaced as the dominant principle of domination but thoroughly *delegitimized* as 'barbaric', 'vulgar' and so on, *except* where they were reshaped and channelled into sanctioned fields in line with the interests of the dominant. The latter include the military and police, as well as the sporting fields, with their close links to the economic field through promotion, advertising and so on. Bourdieu (1984, 1996b, 2004b, 2014; Bourdieu and Passeron, 1990) then, of course, picks up the story to trace the subsequent emergence of contemporary (largely secular) cultural capital and its associated forms of masculinity (reason and *mental* 'strength') over honour as the fundamental principle of class stratification along with economic and social capital.

The physical capital of force, meanwhile, comes to be a possession which, outside of its legitimized fields, operates as a symbolic capital in localized neighbourhood social spaces populated by the dominated, particularly among young men, where it competes against the sanctioned, 'objectified' forms of capital as a means of securing some form of value (being the local 'tough guy' or 'hard man', etc.), however friable, transient and in need of constant maintenance through interpersonal exchanges it might be (see e.g. Sales, 2012). It also continues to act as a source of power within family fields to greater and lesser degrees, most visibly in the form of domestic violence or child abuse as a means of compensating or complementing an individual's positions in other fields but also in a more pervasive and tacit attitude of being 'protective'. That the attributes of physical capital still receive positive cultural representation in certain sections of certain fields of cultural production – films, television programmes and so on focused on 'action heroes' or sports stars – and generates some degree of emulation or seduction is due to the homology between those fields and the social space. The pole oriented towards production for the mass market, aiming to make money and more often comprising agents from families poorer in cultural capital (Bourdieu, 1993b), appeals to their chosen audience by concocting or amplifying stories of valorization and 'making it' without access to the widely legitimated capitals.

We might add to this sketch the parallel development of sexual capital. Ideals of beauty and seduction have long existed, of course, and possibly even functioned more or less systematically as sources of misrecognition at various points in human history (one thinks of ancient Greece, for example), associated with their own arbitrary signifiers. In the modern era, however, it could be argued that they (re)appeared as a *capital* in relation to a specific *field* working through so many localized *markets* with the move from local matrimonial strategies premised on maximization of symbolic and economic capital to elective affinity and attraction as prime principles of pairing with the same changes in communications, transport, education and the occupational structure that brought into being national social spaces of difference (cf. Bourdieu, 2008; Green, 2008; Illouz, 2012). Their value was also likely escalated by heightened sexualization of media and advertising from the mid-twentieth century onwards, i.e. appeal to the specifically sexual channel of the libido in order to sell products of one kind or another, as the product of so many strategies within the (masculine) economic and advertisings fields, as well as by the proliferation of variegated specialists in beauty and sex (therapists, counsellors, beauticians, etc.) charted by Bourdieu (1984). 'Sexiness' thus became something to be not only struggled *over*, with its definition and exchange rate a stake in the field of power, but struggled *for*, as a resource or font of misrecognition, exchangeable with other capitals, in specific fields (modelling, acting, etc.) as well as the more ubiquitous sexual markets (cf. George, 2014). Whether or not the unequal circulation of images and artefacts through the increasingly international chains of symbolic power associated with economic and cultural fields, as well as movements of people, have yet rendered the sexual field more or less global in character, or simply affected the shape and struggles of national or regional fields, is yet to be determined.

A continuing dialectic

If economic capital and cultural capital emerged as preeminent modes of recognition in Western social orders, marginalizing physical capital, and if fields of power have differentiated into the complex mosaics they are today, then how does this shape the way in which gendered social surfaces are currently forged? We have seen how constructions of masculinity and femininity are entwined with struggles over physical capital and sexual capital, but how do they draw from and pattern the capitals defining *class* in contemporary capitalist social orders? Bourdieu's critics think his view on this is pretty straightforward: gender can be reduced down to class, and certainly has no impact of its own on class positioning (e.g. Anthias, 2001). It might be counter-argued, however, that a Bourdieusian understanding already contains the core insight from the influential feminist scholarship on 'intersectionality' – that is, the notion that gender interplays with and refracts other modes of domination – while advancing over it in at least two ways. On the one hand, it breaks with the Marxist view of class in terms of production, exploitation and employment which pervades much intersectional theory, albeit implicitly at times. On the other, as suggested by Krais (1993, 2006), it inexorably expands the 'matrix of domination', to use Patricia Hill Collins' (2000) phrase, beyond the classic triad of gender–class–ethnicity (sometimes squared with age; e.g. Bradley, 1996) to encompass *all* relatively autonomous nexuses of domination in a social order, i.e., fields, both large, like the field of power, and small, like the fields of particular schools, firms and families (Bourdieu, 2001: 102).

The major benefit of shifting from Marx to Bourdieu is the move away from a materialist conception of philosophical anthropology, in which labour is the be-all and end-all of the human condition, towards the vision premised on recognition and misrecognition. The latter neatly avoids any inconsistency in giving equal pegging to modes of

domination other than that of class – a vexation which eventually drove some Marxist feminists to post-Marxism (see
Atkinson, 2015b). In conceiving class as a multidimensional
social space defined by possession of economic, cultural and
social capital, and the differential distance from necessity
they grant, rather than a system of production relations or
occupations, moreover, it sidesteps the tired old debates over
whether and how homemakers, or anyone not in paid work,
can be included and located in the class structure (Atkinson,
2009). There are those who would not believe it: some of
Bourdieu's critics see the social space as essentially a structure of male positions from which women are barred (e.g.
McCall, 1992; Lovell, 2000). Yet that seems to be based
on the faulty assumption that if women were objects of
exchange in Kabylia – which we have already somewhat
de-emphasized – or are agents of capital accumulation for
men in differentiated Western societies (maintaining networks, hosting dinners with the boss, etc.), then they are
unable to possess capitals of their own. There is no logical
necessity of that at all: both men and women possess their
own capital stocks plotting them in social space, some of
which, dependent upon the state of play within the family
field, will be provided by proxy capital made available
through a partner or significant other.

That being the case, how exactly do gender and class
interrelate? The answer, as with many things, is *dialectically*.
On the one hand, the social space is one field – albeit a
major one – not only, as we have already alluded to, shaping
the interests people have in putting forward certain visions
of gender, contributing to the symbolic struggle, but refracting the way in which gendered practices and ideas (including
physicality and sexual attractiveness) are perceived, valued
and embodied. Hence Bourdieu's (1984: 107–8) famous
assertion that there are as many ways of realizing femininity
(and, we would add, masculinity) as there are class positions, and his acknowledgment (Bourdieu, 2001: 93) that
possession of economic, cultural and social capital equip
women with differential capacity to deal with and challenge

masculine domination in the workplace or at home and, perhaps, the symbolic mastery and distance from necessity to play with and resist gendered expectations – whether in relation to jobs, education or modes of dressing and acting – in the way celebrated by Butler. On the other hand, however, what Bourdieu did not make clear enough is that the embodied dispositions, desires and expectations of masculinity and femininity produced by an individual's place within circuits of symbolic power and other fields – the sense of the possible and the impossible, the desirable and the undesirable – *delimit the set of objectively possible and thus thinkable positions, moves and interests within the social space.* It is not, therefore, just a question of 'flavouring' the dispositions and experiences of different zones of social space. It is also a case of differentiating the regions and echelons of social space – or, in terms closer to everyday experience, specific jobs, careers and partnerings – entering consciousness as attainable and attractive, and the consciousness of others advising on, or with power over, one's trajectory as suitable or not (i.e. sexism), and, with that, *likely capital returns and distance from necessity.* A gendered social surface acts as a kind of 'sorting mechanism', to use Erik Olin Wright's (2001) phrase – Bourdieu (2001: 93) himself calls it a 'negative symbolic coefficient' – and is, as such, and contrary to Anthias' (2001: 842) claim, 'constitutive of material positionality' within the Bourdieusian scheme, even though it is not a capital in itself nor an axis of social space (Skeggs, 1997: 101).

Much of this sorting, or filtering, hinges on the mediation of the family and the educational system, both of which operate to channel libidos towards certain fields and split practical and symbolic mastery, and the expectations and projects that go with them, into gendered variants. Amongst those with little in the way of economic and cultural capital, for example, who turn to what they do have as their source of recognition and value – their body or practical skill – there are oppositions between, on the one hand, desires and dispositions for 'hardness' (physical capital) and, on the other, orientations towards glamorous beauty (sexual capital) or committed motherhood (the affective recognition of the family field), plus the opposition between the pursuit of manual trades such as plumbing and so on and personal or caring services like hairdressing, childcare and such like (see Bourdieu, 1993c: 127; 2005a; Archer et al., 2007a, 2007b). Amongst those with ample cultural capital, on the other hand, there is an opposition between the masculine 'hard' sciences aimed at rational mastery or apprenticeships for public power (business studies, political science) and (symbolically devalued and less remunerated) feminine 'soft' sciences, auxiliary medicine, languages and arts as bastions for care, empathy, communication and welfare (Bourdieu and Passeron, 1979, 1990: 78, 183; for recent UK figures, see Office for National Statistics, 2010: 33).

Not only that, but, as is well known (again for figures, see Office for National Statistics, 2010: 37–9), girls tend to outperform boys in education, at least up until the very highest levels of training (i.e. doctorate level). The argument proffered by Bourdieu, and many others, is that this is because certain dispositions (conformity, docility) conducive to a level of school success are historically constructed as 'feminine' – as evidenced in the disparagement of effort by both dominant and dominated boys (Willis, 1977; Aggleton, 1987; Mac an Ghaill, 1994; Epstein et al., 1998; Bourdieu, 2001, 2007: 99–100) – and, therefore, are disproportionately expected of, and thence embodied by, those who perceive themselves as female. That may be, but educational research suggests a more precise explanation: those who are categorized as boys are, from the very start, expected and encouraged to be interested primarily in outdoor, physical games and 'rough and tumble' – with parents interpreting their reactions to different activities as indicating these nascent interests and desires to be catered to – in line with the general, naturalized association of masculinity with physical capital (Siraj and Mayo, 2014). This is the case *even within families rich in cultural capital*, though to a lesser degree than in dominated-class families, and it means boys are less likely than girls to play number and word games with, be read to by, and even just converse with their parents in everyday life – in other words, for activities which intentionally or unintentionally accumulate cultural capital to be a source of affective capital. This is just one reason why, in the latest twist in the tale of gendered categories being associated in perception with different capitals throughout history (demonstrating their arbitrary character), the pole of social space richer in cultural than economic capital, following the feminization of the workforce from the later twentieth century onwards, increasingly tends to be populated disproportionately by women, especially in the middle and dominated classes (see Atkinson, forthcoming b). Thence has followed a contemporary conflation of relative symbolic mastery and cultural capital, even when possessed by men, with perceptions of femininity and effeminacy, feeding back into children's and parents' perceptions of appropriate and normal behaviour.

On leaving education men and women filter into the different layers and sections of the social space their inherited and accrued capital opens up to them, but also into different fields in the field of power, and different sectors of those fields, at different rates (on the university field, for example, see Bourdieu, 1988). Historically, as McNay (1999) and Adkins (2003) have noted, the recent story has been of the increased permeation of the field of power by women thanks to the expanded education system and women's movement, amongst other things, granting access to previously unavailable sources of power. As we have already broached, this has brought all kinds of consequences for the recasting of doxic constructions of and expectations around gender, i.e. 'what women can do', demonstrating the dialectical relation between the prevailing schemata of perception and practice. Whereas once women's libidos tended to be directed by doxic expectations primarily towards the family field rather than fields of cultural, ideological or economic production, in other words, this is now less the case (Bourdieu, 2001; cf. Walby, 1997). On the other hand, not only do gender dispositions and expectations tend – to different degrees in different fields – to result in those classified as men and those as women being distributed into different sectors of those fields (often perceived as different 'branches', 'genres' or 'specialisms') by differentiating their possession of the capital valued within them (cf. Moi, 1991; Krais, 2006). On the whole, the fields making up the field of power still continue to be dominated by men, as well as those hailing from the dominant class (and ethnicity), meaning that the practices and categories of thought produced within and circulated out of them – whether as laws, sermons, medical or teaching practices, etc. – that are misrecognized as legitimate, even if facing a greater heterodoxy, continue to be laden with the schemes of perception of the dominant gender. When taken together with the fact that this domination feeds, through its circuits of symbolic power, in to all the multitude of smaller fields outside of the field of power – workplaces, schools and, crucially, families – then it is clear that this is, ultimately, how 'patriarchy', a word Bourdieu rarely used, can be conceived in contemporary capitalist societies.

Gender and the everyday world

There is another consequence of the continuing feminization of the workforce in the later twentieth century and beyond – one which would, in fact, be hard to spot were we to stick strictly to Bourdieu's own habitual *modus operandi*. Increasingly, as the steady stream of research on 'work–life balance' has amply demonstrated (the classic in the field being Hochschild, 1989), and as McNay (1999) has explicitly suggested without drawing out the broader conceptual ramifications, women's lifeworlds – women's everyday experiences and, consequently, their social surfaces – have come to be defined not just by their positions in particular fields, as key as that is, but by *tension between fields*, specifically the familial field and the fields relating to work, the latter including larger-scale fields (of science or politics, for example, or the bureaucratic field) as well as specific employing organizations and firms (a company, university, etc.). Long experienced in its own way by men, each field, in the manifold ways it manifests in the demands, pressures and releases of ordinary life, competes for the individual's distinctly human desire for recognition, each vies for attention in the stream of consciousness throughout the day, week and so on, each prompts projects which need to be worked out in relation to one another ('prioritizing'), each even affects the position and possible strategies in the others (affecting one's capacity to win capital) and each, ultimately, feeds into a general trans-field sense of probables, i.e. the world horizon.

Some, in the face of these cross-cutting forces, opt to give up or de-prioritize paid work, some decide not to partner and/or have children, in each case sacrificing accumulation of one capital for another, with greater and lesser success, and greater and lesser emotional strain, while others try to balance them in some way. Far from being a simple question of personal 'preference', as Hakim (2000) has it, feeding into the genesis of those strategies will be all sorts of factors, including class-refracted libidinal charge (e.g. work never having had the same appeal as family on account of the types of job available), constraint (expectations of dominant others within the family, the need for money, etc.), efforts at compensation (throwing oneself into one field to battle lack of recognition in the other), discrimination (colleagues presuming family comes first for women, or that they are not as 'rational' as men, and denying them opportunities on that basis) and so on, and the general state of the relationship between the fields across the populace appears to vary according to national policy regimes on childcare, flexible working and so on (Crompton and Lyonette, 2006; cf. Esping-Andersen, 1990).

This felt tension between familial fields and the fields of work, it should be stressed, is not quite the same thing as Dorothy Smith's (1987, 1990) famous notion of 'bifurcated consciousness'. Smith's argument is that there is an experiential cleavage between, on the one hand, the everyday world in all its particularity and singularity – looking after children, helping them with homework, doing the washing up, walking the dog and so on – and, on the other, the domains in which the world is conceptualized, written and talked about in abstracting, generalizing, 'extra-local' ways, grinding out the lived specificities of quotidian life situated in time and space yet foisted on the populace as the legitimate way of knowing – law, politics, business and (social) science, for example. The latter is, according to Smith, bound up with the development of corporate capitalism, since corporations, operating over a wide geographical area, needed to develop forms of knowledge (abstract) and methods of organization (texts) which could apply beyond specific locations and regions in order to maximize profits and efficiency. Since there is an explicit Marxist tint to Smith's vision of the 'relations of ruling', extra-local knowledge is, therefore, a kind of class ideology. Yet it is also a distinctly male world-view, stamped by the interests and orientations of men, in part because members of the dominant class tend to be men, but also because men have the conditions to think abstractly about how things work beyond the everyday, since women usually think about and deal with the everyday – the housework, the children's homework and so on – for them. This even applies to women's employment: they tend to do the mundane clerical, administrative or social service work that keeps the system going rather than the conceptual labour. Hence women experience bifurcated consciousness and have a special insight: their practice sustains the system while they themselves are excluded from its conceptualizing function, and so they can see that the concepts generated via the latter bear little resemblance to what actually goes on. Hence also Smith's suggested solution was to make the everyday world of women the starting point of investigation (or the 'problematic'), not the abstractions of social science; to begin from the problems and pressures of concretely located specific individuals and work out how they are knitted into the circuits constituting the relations of ruling (including the flow of capital and extra-local thinking), not try to cram them into pre-formed categories.

Smith's work does have the virtue of highlighting how consciousness – core and periphery, theme and horizon – can be split between different fields and, more generally, points in the direction of lifeworld analysis with the focused effort to unpack the total constitution of an individual's situation via the chains of social relations leading off from it over time and space to numerous antagonists involved in the production of dominant worldviews. There may even be some parallels between Smith's notion of abstract extra-local knowledge and symbolic mastery. Yet relational phenomenology offers a much sharper conceptual armoury for making sense of all that rightly bothers Smith. First, the switch from Marxism (sometimes with a functionalist gloss, e.g. Smith, 1987: 160) as the means of conceptualizing class struggle to Bourdieu's vision of social space and the field of power gives a more nuanced model for understanding the genesis and dissemination of orthodox and heterodox schemes of perception and categories of thought. The development of extra-local knowledges and their textual forms of mediation are the product of so many conjoined and cross-cutting struggles within the intellectual field, economic field, political field and so on, between players keen to secure recognition in the eyes of others – struggles which tend to run along class and gender (and ethnic) lines, of course, though with their own relative autonomy. Second, consciousness is, strictly speaking, not just *bifurcated* in the instances Smith describes but spread over *multiple* fields related to paid employment, including the social space and symbolic space, giving a more precise and complex picture of the determination of the phenomenology of everyday life, even if the tussle between two fields in particular may be especially salient for the individual. Third, and related to the last point, the split identified by Smith in the case of women being torn between work-based modes of knowledge and practice and the quotidian business of looking after children and home is not really a fissure between 'everyday life' – which one would take to be synonymous with the lifeworld – and fields related to work, but *between fields related to work and the family field*, with 'everyday life', or the lifeworld, encompassing the combination of forces emanating from *all* fields in which the individual is positioned as well as some they are not. Everyday life and the 'relations of ruling', or the field of power, are, in other words, falsely counterposed. It is not a case of men being cut off from the travails of everyday life while women drown in them, therefore, but of the forces of and tensions between specific fields being experienced differently by men and women in their lifeworlds.

Finally, Smith's epistemological principles – the disavowal of abstract categories, starting inquiry with the individual's situation, privileging the agent's everyday perspective – need to be recast. The suspicion of the categories of thought produced by the relations of ruling is, without a doubt, justified, and indeed runs along the same tracks as Bourdieu's Bachelardian insistence on bracketing out prenotions and spontaneous sociology, both of which can be vehicles for mystifying and sustaining power. Yet even if we want to begin with the individual's situation *in toto*, as in lifeworld analysis, we have to acknowledge that sociology is itself, inescapably, a symbolic/sign system demanding a certain mastery and that, consequently, perception is theory laden (Smith's generalizing theory of the relations of ruling, and her application of this model to all her case studies, demonstrates all this). It is not possible, therefore, to disregard abstraction altogether, but we can exercise epistemological vigilance, subject ourselves to thoroughgoing reflexivity to try to iron out the prejudices born of our position and interests in the intellectual field and proceed to construct a reasoned model of the object under investigation. Furthermore, while people's experience can throw a structural tension into sharp relief and act as a useful starting point of inquiry, and while people can often have a practical grasp of some of the principles of their practice, they have their own prenotions, their own spontaneous views of the world adjusted to their positions in the world, and so to make full sense of their experience, their practical knowledge and their prenotions, we need to go beyond their standpoint using the kind of reason made possible, even if in competition with other forces, by the historical development of the scientific field.

Recapitulation

It is true that Bourdieu (1997b: 190) himself claimed not to be interested in 'huge and vague' questions such as 'what gender is' or how it intersects with other forms of division and domination, choosing instead to remain close to his concrete analysis of masculine domination in Kabylia. Sticking with this particular case, however, and attempting to smuggle answers to those big questions in by the back door, so to speak, has not only generated some misunderstanding, amongst both critics and more or less sympathetic appropriators, but stopped Bourdieu from pushing a little bit deeper, or in fresh directions, on certain questions – sexual attraction and the historical genesis of gender domination, for example. Bourdieu's toolkit is often discarded quicker than it should be as a result, sometimes at second hand, yet it also means that those who are inspired by Bourdieu, who find his work compelling but follow the letter rather than the spirit of his writings, end up positing problematic concepts that, in turn, are easy to find fault with and lead critics to see the whole programme as best avoided.

Whilst hardly able to claim to have provided definitive conclusions, rather than merely hypotheses and starting points, I have opted instead to engage the major issues head on and explore solutions which adhere to the philosophical core of Bourdieu's approach but push in the direction of relational phenomenology. Thus I have clarified that gender is, at root, a perceptual-linguistic categorization uniting, dividing and mobilizing people and practices. It is organized around a relational polarity, defining one pole as not the other, though this gives scope for a blending of elements in everyday practice and genesis of categories for making sense of varying degrees of 'hybridity'. Moreover, far from being completely doxic and efficiently reproduced, it is struggled over within the various fields comprising the field of power in line with the interests that prevail there, with the competing definitions thence disseminated to different degrees depending on different levels of symbolic capital along different time-space circuits into individual lifeworlds within a social order. There the constructions and their associated symbols and signs are encountered, read and incorporated according to the individual's positions in *numerous* fields, including the social space, the sexual field, fields involving physical capital, the micro-fields of mundane life and, as a special case, the family field. Struggles within all of these fields over what is masculine and feminine, manly and unmanly, girly or butch, right and wrong then feed back into the struggles and practices of the field of power, in dialectical fashion, via representatives and homologues. The sexual field and physical capital, as well as the social space, have particular clout in this regard, their stakes being so closely entwined with constructions of masculine and feminine corporeality and capacity through history that they are misrecognized as inherently connected. At the same time, we have to go beyond Bourdieu and recognize, as feminists have pointed out, that many of the stressful tensions and painful privations of gendered experience in contemporary Western social orders, if not beyond, relate to the conflict between multiple fields – their tug on the libido, their competition for attention, the assumptions made by others over one's level of commitment to either – within the everyday lifeworld. Only then will we be able to fully document, and fight against, the suffering caused – for women and men – by androcentrism.

Epilogue: Sketch of a Research Programme

Nothing posited in the foregoing is contrary to the fundamental philosophical keystones of Bourdieu's sociology – relationalism, recognition, sociologized rationalism. Indeed in most cases the concepts and elaborations offered have built on implicit assumptions or highly suggestive yet all-too-brief comments across Bourdieu's own corpus. Nonetheless, by extracting and working through the notions of world (from habitat) and circuits of symbolic power (from legitimation chains), and elucidating their relation to fields and habitus, particularly via the concepts of social surface and world horizon, the way has been cleared, I hope, for the analysis of phenomena overlooked or marginalized in Bourdieu's own research. This is, after all, what concepts should be for: to serve as tools, mobilized in specific programmes of research, for making sense of the social world.

On the one hand, then, with circuits of symbolic power recovered from the margins of Bourdieu's *oeuvre*, space has been opened up for analysis of the differential dispersal and impact, across time and geography, of objects, practices and categories of thought springing from field struggles, including those originating within the state *qua* bureaucratic field, thus filling in the gaps on genesis, struggle, appropriation, symbolic violence and dissemination power acknowledged in investigations of 'innovation diffusion' by Hägerstrand (1967) but also haunting perspectives as diverse as governmentality studies and globalization theory. Global supply chains, the geographical distribution of commodities/bodies/ ideas, spatial divisions of labour, territorial jurisdictions, information flows, uses of social media and so on, while merely partially understood if one field and its 'epistemic individuals' are in focus, can be the object of sociological construction too, but they only make sense when seen in dialectical relation with the structures of a multitude of interacting spaces of contention for specific forms of recognition.

On the other hand, with the notion of habitat reworked as lifeworld and family relations conceived as a field, the possibilities have expanded for exploration of the individual *qua* 'total being', as Mauss put it, with a distinct social surface, and their everyday life as the centre point of multiple determinations; of particular situations and junctures, institutionalized or not, as the aggregate outcome of multiple forces; and of the channelling and (im)balance, in quotidian experience, of an individual's desires and attention between multiple fields. Phenomenology places to the fore the mundane experience of the world as a whole and the genesis of the knowledge-disposition complexes that make us who we are, but Bourdieu allows us to locate that world and that genesis within so many structural relations. As the stream of thematic and peripheral consciousness slips between work tasks, desire for a certain consumer good, concern about a specific bill, sexual fantasy, the family day out at the weekend and so on in the flow of everyday events or via a chain of association, to different degrees at different times and spaces and depending on the strength of one's 'balance of investments', it surges between so many structured spaces of possibility and struggle, plugging in to and out of one or more at a time. Yet Bourdieu failed to appreciate that practice and position-taking in relation to one field is generated not *just* by one's position within that field but, by virtue of the world horizon, by the state of play in others drawing the individual's libido too.

None of this is to say that the study of specific fields, and the isolation of particular pertinent features for mapping their fundamental structure and history, is to be done away with. That remains a basic task for the Bourdieu-inspired. A fruitful way forward may, instead, be to systematically *pair* field analysis and lifeworld analysis, each filling in what the other puts in analytical parentheses. One may well want to chart, for example, the general structure of a field not studied before by Bourdieu – the military field or medical field, say. Through correspondence analysis and other methods, one can document the system of oppositions in position-takings and power relations, the field's place in relation to the field of power and its homology with class. One may even want to go a little further than Bourdieu did and study the chains of symbolic power distributing field effects, in the form of specific goods or events, over time and space to implicated players as well as those beyond the field – 'insurgents' in other lands, or patients, for instance – and the factors affecting their spatio-temporal reach. Yet one can also, to add to this, switch regard to examine the relative place of the focal field in individual lives. This would encompass, first of all, exploration of how the family, locale, school, political and media representations and so on combined to forge the masteries, dispositions, entry-ticket capitals and, crucially, the *desire* to become a soldier or medical professional in the first place, and to be one of a certain *type* relative to others. Yet it would also foreground how the forces of the military or medical field are (im)balanced against the demands and determinations of other fields in the individual's lifeworld, whether the family, the sexual field (manifesting as harassment or lust, for example), the social and symbolic spaces or the specific employer or institution funnelling the larger field's determinations, perhaps even with the effect, potentially disillusioning and painful, of weakening or overruling the *libido medicina* or *militaris* and generating the ultimate strategy of field exit. Or one can examine how the nexus between social space and family, and with that between the social space and gender, pans out in different nations according to the indigenous field of power and its place in the global space of power struggles. The point is that field analysis and lifeworld analysis are not antagonistic. Each is only a change of analytical focus, a way of viewing and approaching the same social ontology, a temporary 'bracketing', in the Giddensian sense, of either lifeworlds or full field structures. Field analysis will enrich the study of lifeworlds as much as vice versa, and should remain a bedrock of any future research programme in relational phenomenology, but it should not be the sole legacy of Bourdieu's rich corpus for social science.

Notes

1. Introduction

1. This study can be thought of as the empirical or 'applied' counterpart to the current volume, much as Bourdieu's *The Logic of Practice* (1990b) served as a distillation of the theoretical lessons of *Distinction* (1984).
2. Boltanski's (2011) programme focuses on how 'actors' negotiate disputes *in situ*, identifying and criticizing an injustice by virtue of one regime of justification or worth, or 'polity', invading a practice supposedly revolving around another (e.g. matters of class culture invading considerations of university entry). Yet one is constantly left wondering why one polity invades another and why (certain) others consider it unjust – whose *interests* does the injustice serve, whose interests does its overthrow serve, and why do they have those divergent interests in the first place?

2. The Lifeworld

1. The positing of these micro-fields deflates the criticism that Bourdieu lacks a sufficient means for analysing the operation of institutions (Jenkins, 2002).
2. Time geographers have, to their credit, acknowledged the ways in which their particular way of looking at the world and

phenomenology may complement each other, and they even share some basic assumptions (projection, the present as summation of the past, etc.), but the interface has always been fairly superficial. See particularly Lenntorp (1976, 1999) and Pred (1981a).

3. Lest the specific example provoke charges of lapsing into the 'scholastic point of view', substitute 'conference plenary' and 'intellectual field' with 'exhibition' and 'artistic field', 'business meeting' and 'economic field', 'concert' and 'the field of amateur brass bands' (Dubois et al., 2013), and so on.

4. Bourdieu (1996b: 271) did recognize the existence of this multiplicity of practice, but not its broader significance.

5. When discussing the differential power of companies within the economic field to construct and utilize distribution networks, Bourdieu (2005a) coined the term 'commercial capital', but it could be argued that, as in other fields, such power over dissemination is actually reducible to economic and (in the form of recognition of the 'name' or 'brand') social capital.

6. Urry's (2007) notion of 'network capital', built on the same premise of turning spatial processes into a capital, is as problematic as mobility capital. It is impossible to see how most of its eight supposed elements – resources allowing mobility, others at-a-distance, possession of information and contact points (diaries, phones, etc.), possession of communications devices, access to meeting areas, access to technologies of mobility and time – are not ultimately reducible to, or rather *products of*, economic, cultural and social capital and the conditions of existence they bring. His example of Hurricane Katrina, from which the economically rich could escape while the urban poor were left to suffer, reinforces that impression.

7. This is, to be fair, the direction Kaufmann, an advocate of mobility capital, seems to have gone in his later work, but others continue to use the term nonetheless (e.g. Carlson, 2013).

8. Whatever his exaggerations on cosmopolitanism, Beck's (2000) notion of 'place polygamy' captures the phenomenology of this rootedness in more than one social/symbolic space, i.e. the world horizon: the sense of investment in different social games, with different systems of oppositions,

which may harmonize or clash in different ways and recipro-
cally affect one's desire and capacity to accumulate capital in
either.

3. The Field of Family Relations

1. Bourdieu does not, as Silva (2005) argues, presuppose or natu-
   ralize the nuclear family, therefore, but rather provides tools
   for the examination of the socio-historical processes through
   which it has *become* presupposed and naturalized in *everyday*
   perception.
2. While followers of the quasi-ethnomethodological 'family
   practice' theory espoused by Morgan (1996) and popular in
   the UK often document patent struggles over symbolic capital
   (the power to decree what should be done) and love – for
   example, Allan et al.'s (2011) study of step-families – they fail
   to see them as such and thus obfuscate their underlying genetic
   principle to the extent that domestic antagonism appears to
   emerge *ex nihilo*. In Allan et al.'s case, this is exacerbated
   by their definition of love in terms of 'enduring solidarity'
   (which points more to specific family doxa) rather than as a
   specific, primary form of *recognition*, *misrecognition* and thus
   capital, the differential possession of which puts members in
   different objective and subjective relations to one another and
   generates manifold affective responses and lines of action (i.e.
   strategies).
3. Though couples are often brought together by elective affinity
   (Bourdieu, 1984), this is only ever to greater and lesser degrees
   and will depend upon a whole range of forces within the lifeworld, not least orientation towards sexual capital, the balance
   of the libido between fields and the possibilities for encounter
   provided by spatial location and motility.
4. That the qualifier 'like' places childminders, nannies, etc., in
   a particular perceptual relation vis-à-vis the other perceived
   members of the 'family', and that this relationship can be
   a fundamental source of the negotiation of class and ethnic
   differences within the familial field, has been shown by
   O'Connell (2010).
5. This is a refinement of my earlier argument, wherein the
   family universe (the full system of interrelations between
   fields) and constellations (specific clusters of fields within the

universe) were conflated, hopefully not pushing the astronomical analogy too far.

4. Social Becoming

1. These latter points are the site of interconnection between phenomenological and structuralist approaches to knowledge and may find a bridge in a reworking of Husserl's (fairly obscure) notion of 'relative determination' in which a single percept is intuited according to its place vis-à-vis a collection (or *system*) of other percepts. This is not, in any case, the simple associationism of empiricism and behaviourism. Association of disparate ideas and signs on the basis of bare contiguity in experience (as well as homophony, metaphor, etc.) does occur, of course, and has its effect on the stream of consciousness, but the *significance* of ideas and signs is nevertheless organized around distinct relational structures provided by fields which are themselves defined relative to one another in the individual's lived experience, such that the association leads attention *between* field pertinences. A political event that occurred while writing this book may pop into my head when I think of the book, but the pertinence of both the political event and the book are defined by my position and relative illusio vis-à-vis the social space (and its homology with the space of political position-takings) and the intellectual/sociological field.

2. Just as genetic phenomenology finds its neurological correlate in the formation, activation and strengthening/weakening of synaptic connections, the concept of libido, far from being some mystical force, has a distinct neurological correlate in the existence and structured flow through neural circuits of certain neurotransmitters (noradrenaline, dopamine, serotonin, etc.).

3. At the level of philosophical anthropology, this is what makes recognition the bedrock rather than material struggles (Marxism) or interdependency (Elias): only because the parent recognizes the child as worthy or valuable – i.e. as a being capable of (eventually) giving to or garnering for the caregiver some form of recognition in return – do they feed them, clothe them, wash them, etc.

4. The 'mirror' and 'specular' image need not be literal – they are merely metaphors for the nature of development at this stage, which happens to be most tangible in relation to actual mirrors. Recognition of oneself also comes via responses of caregivers to one's vocalizations and gestures (Steinmetz, 2014).

5. The thematization of 'self' or 'ego', which is nothing more than the representation of oneself relative to others in one or multiple struggles for recognition (as a man, white British, and such like or as stupid, ugly, worthless, etc.), can feed into deliberated, projected activity and post-hoc rationalization (the in-order-to motive), e.g. 'it's not for me/my thing'. Some scholars would label this 'reflexivity', though given the multitude of meanings that term has acquired in sociology I prefer to reserve it for the process of participant objectivation, as Bourdieu did. More spontaneous activity of the kind Bourdieu tends to (over)emphasize, which Mead (1934) sees as the 'I' in action and Freud as the 'id' or the unconscious, is still based on a socially conditioned sense of what can and what must be done in relation to one or more struggles for recognition given one's place (the because motive), but a sense of self is not thematic.

6. They only *contribute* to the sense of the possible, alongside time-space location and motility, rather than exclusively generate it, as social network theory erroneously has it. This will be picked up later.

7. Compare the 'glitches and ruptures' recognized by Reay et al. (2005: 71), and the rich analyses of familial relations produced by Archer (2012), both of which actually contradict the authors' explicit theoretical frameworks (Atkinson, 2011a, 2013). Corsaro (2015: 167) also draws attention to how imitation among older children, far from being a simple mimesis, as Bourdieu had it, is often elaborated and embellished in line with their own position and interests in the field – teasing an adult to win their recognition, or mocking them as a mode of defence.

5. Gender

1. This is, as it happens, the reverse of what I have argued for in the case of ethno-racial/national domination (Atkinson,

2015a). Whereas Wacquant (2014) is of the view that race does not form a field of its own because it is a scheme of perception, and habitus, rooted in *all* fields, Bourdieu (1991) has suggested and Hage (1998) has demonstrated that it is analytically fruitful and coherent to conceive ethno-racial/national domination in contemporary 'multicultural' social orders as a relatively autonomous space of struggle, with its own forms of symbolic capital, homologous with the social space and other fields. Part of the difference here stems from the fact that Wacquant, perhaps misled by the prevailing prenotions of US culture and law, unhelpfully reduces race to a black/white binary analogous to gender and keeps it distinct from ethnicity/nationalism.

2. Of course, even this statement, like all deductions and theories deemed 'scientific' (i.e. that meet criteria established in the field of science), is a construction of the object insofar as it uses language and models forged through social struggles within pertinent intersecting fields. Yet, as outlined in chapter 1, Bourdieu's epistemology and sociology of science (as presented in Bourdieu, 2004a; Bourdieu et al., 1991) remain realist at their cores. There may be no unmediated access to reality, but, as the critical realists have done most to elaborate (on Kantian foundations), that does not mean there is no unchanging reality *anchoring* those models and, in Bachelardian vein, allowing the clearing away of errors. In Bhaskar's (1989: 11) words, there is simply 'changing knowledge of unchanged objects'.

References

Abrahams, J. and Ingram, N. (2013) 'The Chameleon Habitus: Exploring Local Students' Negotiations of Multiple Fields'. *Sociological Research Online*, 18 (4): 21.

Adkins, L. (2003) 'Reflexivity: Freedom or Habit of Gender?'. *Theory, Culture and Society*, 20 (6): 21–42.

Adkins, L. and Skeggs, B. (Eds.) (2004) *Feminism After Bourdieu*. Oxford: Blackwell.

Aggleton, P. (1987) *Rebels Without a Cause?* London: Falmer.

Alanen, L. (2011) 'Capitalizing on Family', in L. Alanen and M. Siisiänen (Eds.) *Fields and Capitals: Constructing Local Life*. Jyväskylä: University of Jyväskylä Press, pp. 91–123.

Alanen, L. and Mayall, B. (Eds.) (2001) *Conceptualizing Child–Adult Relations*. London: Routledge.

Alanen, L., Brooker, L. and Mayall, B. (Eds.) (2015) *Childhood with Bourdieu*. Basingstoke: Palgrave Macmillan.

Alexander, J. (1995) *Fin de Siècle Social Theory*. London: Verso.

Allan, G. and Crow, G. (Eds.) (1989) *Home and Family*. Basingstoke: Macmillan.

Allan, G. and Crow, G. (2001) *Families, Households and Society*. Basingstoke: Palgrave Macmillan.

Allan, G., Crow, G. and Hawker, S. (2011) *Stepfamilies*. Basingstoke: Palgrave Macmillan.

Allatt, P. (1993) 'Becoming Privileged: The Role of Family Processes', in I. Bates and G. Riseborough (Eds.) *Youth and Inequality*. Buckingham: Open University Press, pp. 139–59.

Anthias, F. (2001) 'The Concept of "Social Division" and Theorising Social Stratification'. *Sociology*, 35 (4): 835–54.

Archer, L., Halsall, A. and Hollingworth, S. (2007a) 'Class, Gender, (Hetero)Sexuality and Schooling'. *British Journal of Sociology of Education*, 28 (2): 165–80.

Archer, L., Hollingworth, S. and Halsall, A. (2007b) ' "University's not for Me – I'm a Nike Person": Urban, Working-Class Young People's Negotiations of "Style", Identity and Educational Engagement'. *Sociology*, 41 (2): 219–37.

Archer, M. (2007) *Making Our Way Through the World: Human Reflexivity and Social Mobility*. Cambridge: Cambridge University Press.

Archer, M. (2012) *The Reflexive Imperative in Late Modernity*. Cambridge: Cambridge University Press.

Ariès, P. (1996) *Centuries of Childhood* (new edn). London: Pimlico.

Armengaud, F., Jasser, G. and Delphy, C. (1995) 'Liberty, Equality . . . But Most of All Fraternity'. *Trouble and Strife*, 31: 43–9.

Atkinson, W. (2009) 'Rethinking the Work–Class Nexus'. *Sociology*, 43 (5): 896–912.

Atkinson, W. (2010a) *Class, Individualization and Late Modernity: In Search of the Reflexive Worker*. Basingstoke: Palgrave Macmillan.

Atkinson, W. (2010b) 'Phenomenological Additions to the Bourdieusian Toolbox: Two Problems for Bourdieu, Two Solutions from Schutz'. *Sociological Theory*, 28 (1): 1–19.

Atkinson, W. (2011a) 'From Sociological Fictions to Social Fictions: Some Bourdieusian Reflections on the Concepts of "Institutional Habitus" and "Family Habitus"'. *British Journal of Sociology of Education*, 32 (3): 331–47.

Atkinson, W. (2011b) 'The Context and Genesis of Musical Tastes: Omnivorousness Debunked, Bourdieu Buttressed'. *Poetics*, 39 (3): 169–86.

Atkinson, W. (2012) '*Reproduction* Revisited: Comprehending Complex Educational Trajectories'. *The Sociological Review*, 60 (4): 734–52.

Atkinson, W. (2013) 'Review of *The Reflexive Imperative in Late Modernity*'. *European Journal of Social Theory*, 7 (1): 122–6.

Atkinson, W. (2015a) 'Putting Habitus Back in its Place?'. *Body and Society*, 21 (4): 103–16.

Atkinson, W. (2015b) *Class*. Cambridge: Polity.

Atkinson, W. (forthcoming a) 'Bourdieu and Schutz: Bringing Together Two Sons of Husserl', in J. Sallaz and T. Medvetz (Eds.) *The Oxford Handbook of Pierre Bourdieu*. Oxford: Oxford University Press.

Atkinson, W. (forthcoming b) *Class in the New Millennium: Structure, Homologies and Experience in Contemporary Britain*. London: Routledge.

Bachelard, G. (1994) *The Poetics of Space*. Boston, MA: Beacon Press.

Bacqué, M.-H., Bridge, G., Benson, M., Butler, T., Charmes, E., Fijalkow, Y., Jackson, E., Launay, L. and Vermeersch, S. (2015) *The Middle Classes and the City: A Study of Paris and London*. Basingstoke: Palgrave Macmillan.

Balint, M. (1956) 'Pleasure, Object and Libido'. *British Journal of Medical Psychology*, 29 (2): 162–7.

Bassett, S. (Ed.) (1989) *The Origins of Anglo-Saxon Kingdoms*. Leicester: Leicester University Press.

Beauvoir, S. de (2010) *The Second Sex*. London: Vintage.

Beck, U. (2000) *What is Globalization?* Cambridge: Polity.

Beck, U. (2007) *Cosmopolitan Europe*. Cambridge: Polity.

Beck, U. and Beck-Gernsheim, E. (1995) *The Normal Chaos of Love*. Cambridge: Polity.

Beck, U. and Beck-Gernsheim, E. (2002) *Individualization*. London: Sage.

Beck, U. and Beck-Gernsheim, E. (2014) *Distant Love*. Cambridge: Polity.

Becker, H. (2010) *Art Worlds* (2nd edn). Berkeley, CA: University of California Press.

Benson, R. and Neveu, E. (2005) 'Introduction: Field Theory as a Work in Progress', in R. Benson and E. Neveu (Eds.) *Bourdieu and the Journalistic Field*. Cambridge: Polity, pp. 1–26.

Berger, B. and Berger, P. (1983) *The War over the Family*. London: Hutchinson.

Berger, P. and Kellner, H. (1964) 'Marriage and the Construction of Reality'. *Diogenes*, 12 (46): 1–24.

Berger, P. and Luckmann, T. (1991) *The Social Construction of Reality*. London: Penguin.

Bhaskar, R. (1989) *The Possibility of Naturalism*. London: Routledge.

Boltanski, L. (2011) *On Critique*. Cambridge: Polity.

152   *References*

Bourdieu, P. (1977) *Outline of a Theory of Practice*. Cambridge: Cambridge University Press.

Bourdieu, P. (1979) *Algeria 1960*. Cambridge: Cambridge University Press.

Bourdieu, P. (1984) *Distinction*. London: Routledge.

Bourdieu, P. (1988) *Homo Academicus*. Cambridge: Polity.

Bourdieu, P. (1990a) *The Political Ontology of Martin Heidegger*. Cambridge: Polity.

Bourdieu, P. (1990b) *The Logic of Practice*. Cambridge: Polity.

Bourdieu, P. (1990c) *In Other Words*. Cambridge: Polity.

Bourdieu, P. (1991) 'Epilogue: On the Possibility of a Field of World Sociology', in P. Bourdieu and J. Coleman (Eds.) *Social Theory for a Changing Society*. Boulder, CO: Westview Press, pp. 373–87.

Bourdieu, P. (1993a) 'Concluding Remarks: For a Sociogenetic Understanding of Intellectual Works', in C. Calhoun, E. LiPuma and M. Postone (Eds.) *Bourdieu: Critical Perspectives*. Cambridge: Polity, pp. 263–75.

Bourdieu, P. (1993b) *The Field of Cultural Production*. Cambridge: Polity.

Bourdieu, P. (1993c) *Sociology in Question*. London: Sage.

Bourdieu, P. (1994) 'Stratégies de Reproduction et Modes de Domination'. *Actes de la Recherche en Sciences Sociales*, 105: 3–12.

Bourdieu, P. (1996a) *The Rules of Art*. Cambridge: Polity.

Bourdieu, P. (1996b) *The State Nobility*. Cambridge: Polity.

Bourdieu, P. (1997a) 'Passport to Duke'. *Metaphilosophy*, 28 (4): 449–55.

Bourdieu, P. (1997b) 'Masculine Domination Revisited'. *Berkeley Journal of Sociology*, 41: 189–204.

Bourdieu, P. (1998) *Practical Reason*. Cambridge: Polity.

Bourdieu, P. (1999a) 'The Social Conditions of the International Circulation of Ideas', in R. Shusterman (Ed.) *Bourdieu: A Critical Reader*. Oxford: Blackwell, pp. 220–8.

Bourdieu, P. (1999b) 'Site Effects', in P. Bourdieu et al., *The Weight of the World*. Stanford, CA: Stanford University Press, pp. 123–9.

Bourdieu, P. (1999c) 'The Contradictions of Inheritance', in P. Bourdieu et al., *The Weight of the World*. Stanford: Stanford University Press, pp. 507–13.

Bourdieu, P. (2000a) 'The Biographical Illusion', in P. du Gay, J. Evans and P. Redman (Eds.) *Identity: A Reader.* London: Sage, pp. 297–303.

Bourdieu, P. (2000b) *Pascalian Meditations.* Cambridge: Polity.

Bourdieu, P. (2001) *Masculine Domination.* Cambridge: Polity.

Bourdieu, P. (2002) 'Response to Throop and Murphy'. *Anthropological Theory,* 2 (2): 209.

Bourdieu, P. (2004a) *Science of Science and Reflexivity.* Cambridge: Polity.

Bourdieu, P. (2004b) 'From the King's House to the Reason of State'. *Constellations,* 11 (1): 16–36.

Bourdieu, P. (2005a) *The Social Structures of the Economy.* Cambridge: Polity.

Bourdieu, P. (2005b) 'Habitus', in J. Hillier and E. Rooksby (Eds.) *Habitus: A Sense of Place* (2nd edn). Aldershot: Ashgate.

Bourdieu, P. (2007) *Sketch for a Self-Analysis.* Cambridge: Polity.

Bourdieu, P. (2008) *The Bachelors' Ball.* Cambridge: Polity.

Bourdieu, P. (2013) *Algerian Sketches.* Cambridge: Polity.

Bourdieu, P. (2014) *On the State.* Cambridge: Polity.

Bourdieu, P. and Passeron, J.-C. (1979) *The Inheritors.* Chicago, IL: University of Chicago Press.

Bourdieu, P. and Passeron, J.-C. (1990) *Reproduction in Education, Society and Culture* (2nd edn). London: Sage.

Bourdieu, P. and Wacquant, L.J.D. (1992) *An Invitation to Reflexive Sociology.* Cambridge: Polity.

Bourdieu, P., Chamboredon, J.-C. and Passeron, J.-C. (1991) *The Craft of Sociology.* New York: Walter de Gruyter.

Bowlby, J. (1969) *Attachment and Loss* (Vol. 1). London: Hogarth Press.

Bradley, H. (1996) *Fractured Identities.* Cambridge: Polity.

Bridge, G. (2004) 'Pierre Bourdieu', in P. Hubbard, R. Kitchin and G. Valentine (Eds.) *Key Thinkers in Space and Place.* London: Sage, pp. 69–64.

Bridge, G. (2013) 'A Transactional Perspective on Space'. *International Planning Studies,* 18 (3–4): 304–20.

Bronckart, J.-P. and Shurman, M.-N. (1999) 'Pierre Bourdieu – Jean Piaget', in B. Lahire (Ed.) *Le Travail Sociologique de Pierre Bourdieu.* Paris: La Découverte, pp. 153–78.

Bruner, J. and Haste, H. (Eds.) (1987) *Making Sense.* London: Methuen.

Burguière, A., Klapisch-Zuber, C., Segalen, M. and Zonabend, F. (Eds.) (1996) *A History of the Family* (2 vols). Cambridge: Polity.

Burke, K., Emmerich, N. and Ingram, N. (2013) 'Well-Founded Social Fictions: A Defence of the Concepts of Institutional and Familial Habitus'. *British Journal of Sociology of Education*, 34 (2): 165–82.

Burman, E. (2008) *Deconstructing Developmental Psychology* (2nd edn). London: Routledge.

Carlson, S. (2013) 'Becoming a Mobile Student'. *Population, Space and Place*, 19 (2): 168–80.

Carraher, T., Schliemann, A. and Carraher, D. (1988) 'Mathematical Concepts in Everyday Life', in G. Saxe and M. Gearhart (Eds.) *Children's Mathematics*. San Francisco, CA: Jossey-Bass, pp. 71–87.

Certeau, M. de (1984) *The Practice of Everyday Life*. Berkeley, CA: University of California Press.

Chodorow, N. (1978) *The Reproduction of Mothering*. Berkeley, CA: University of California Press.

Cicourel, A. (1993) 'Aspects of Structural and Processual Theories of Knowledge', in C. Calhoun, E. LiPuma and M. Postone (Eds.) *Bourdieu: Critical Perspectives*. Cambridge: Polity, pp. 89–115.

Cohen, P. (1972) 'Sub-Cultural Conflict and Working Class Community'. *Working Papers in Cultural Studies* 2. Birmingham, CCCS: 5–51.

Coles, T. (2007) 'Negotiating the Field of Masculinity'. *Men and Masculinities*, 12 (1): 30–44.

Collins, P.H. (2000) *Black Feminist Thought* (2nd edn). London: Routledge.

Collins, R. (2004) *Interaction Ritual Chains*. Princeton, NJ: Princeton University Press.

Connell, R. (1983) *Which Way is Up?* London: Allen and Unwin.

Connell, R. (1987) *Gender and Power*. Cambridge: Polity.

Connell, R. (2005) *Masculinities* (2nd edn). Cambridge: Polity.

Connell, R. (2007) *Southern Theory*. Cambridge: Polity.

Connolly, P. (2004) *Boys and Schooling in the Early Years*. London: RoutledgeFalmer.

Corsaro, W. (2015) *The Sociology of Childhood* (4th edn). London: Sage.

Costa, C. (forthcoming) 'Double Gamers: Academics Between Fields'. *British Journal of Sociology of Education*, DOI: 10.1080/01425692.2014.982861.

Crompton, R. and Lyonette, C. (2006) 'Work–Life "Balance" in Europe'. *Acta Sociologica*, 49 (4): 379–93.

Crossley, N. (2002) *Making Sense of Social Movements*. Buckingham: Open University Press.

Crossley, N. (2010) *Toward Relational Sociology*. London: Routledge.

Crossley, N. (2013) 'Interactions, Juxtapositions and Tastes', in C. Powell and F. Dépelteau (Eds.) *Conceptualizing Relational Sociology*. Basingstoke: Palgrave Macmillan, pp. 123–44.

Crossley, N. and Bottero, W. (2011) 'Worlds, Fields and Networks'. *Cultural Sociology*, 5 (1): 99–119.

Davies, K. (2015) 'Siblings, Stories and the Self'. *Sociology*, 49 (4): 670–95.

DeCasper, A.J. and Fifer, W.P. (1980) 'Of Human Bonding: Newborns Prefer Their Mothers' Voices'. *Science*, 208 (4448): 1174–6.

DeLanda, M. (2011) *A New Philosophy of Society*. London: Continuum.

Dépelteau, F. and Powell, C. (Eds.) (2013) *Applying Relational Sociology*. Basingstoke: Palgrave Macmillan.

DeVault, M.L. (1994) *Feeding the Family: The Social Organization of Caring as Gendered Work*. Chicago, IL: University of Chicago Press.

Devine, F. (2004) *Class Practices*. Cambridge: Cambridge University Press.

Dixon, S. (1992) *The Roman Family*. Baltimore, MD: Johns Hopkins University Press.

Dominguez Rubio, F. and Silva, E. (2013) 'Materials in the Field'. *Cultural Sociology*, 7 (2): 161–78.

Donaldson, M. (1978) *Children's Minds*. London: Fontana.

Donzelot, J. (1980) *The Policing of Families: Welfare v the State*. London: Hutchinson.

Dubois, V. (2010) *The Bureaucrat and the Poor*. Farnham: Ashgate.

Dubois, V., Méon, J.-M. and Pierru, E. (2013) *The Sociology of Wind Bands*. Farnham: Ashgate.

Eder, K. (1993) *The New Politics of Class*. London: Sage.

Edwards, R. (2010) 'Parenting Practices and Class', in M. Klett-Davies (Ed.) *Is Parenting a Class Issue?* London: Family and Parenting Institute, pp. 62–76.

Elias, N. (1978) *What is Sociology?* New York: Columbia University Press.

Elias, N. (2000) *The Civilizing Process* (rev. edn). Oxford: Blackwell.

Engels, F. (1986) *The Origins of the Family, Private Property and the State*. London: Penguin.

Epstein, D., Elwood, J., Hey, V. and Maw, J. (Eds) (1998) *Failing Boys? Issues in Gender and Achievement*. Buckingham: Open University Press.

Erikson, E. (1977) *Childhood and Society* (2nd edn). London: Paladin.

Esping-Andersen, G. (1990) *The Three Worlds of Welfare Capitalism*. Cambridge: Polity.

Fairbairn, R. (1952) *Psychoanalytic Studies of the Personality*. London: Tavistock.

Feinman, S. (Ed.) (1992) *Social Referencing and the Social Construction of Reality in Infancy*. New York: Plenum Press.

Finch, J. (1989) *Family Obligations and Social Change*. Cambridge: Polity.

Finch, J. (2007) 'Displaying Families'. *Sociology*, 45 (1): 65–81.

Finch, J. and Mason, J. (1993) *Negotiating Family Responsibilities*. London: Routledge.

Finch, J. and Mason, J. (2000) *Passing On*. London: Routledge.

Flamm, M. and Kaufmann, V. (2006) 'Operationalising the Concept of Motility'. *Mobilities*, 1 (2): 167–89.

Fligstein, N. and McAdam, D. (2011) *A Theory of Fields*. Oxford: Oxford University Press.

Fogle, N. (2011) *The Spatial Logic of Social Struggle: A Bourdieuian Topology*. Lanham, MD: Lexington Books.

Foucault, M. (1982) 'The Subject and Power', in H. Dreyfus and P. Rabinow, *Michel Foucault*. New York: Harvester Wheatsheaf, pp. 208–26.

Fourny, J.-F. (2000) 'Bourdieu's Uneasy Psychoanalysis'. *SubStance*, 29 (3): 103–12.

Fowler, B. (2003) 'Reading Pierre Bourdieu's Masculine Domination: Notes towards an Intersectional Analysis of Gender, Culture and Class'. *Cultural Studies*, 17 (3–4): 468–94.

Freud, A. (1968) *The Ego and the Mechanisms of Defence*. London: Hogarth Press.

Frith, S. (2007) *Taking Popular Music Seriously*. Aldershot: Ashgate.

Garfinkel, H. (1984) *Studies in Ethnomethodology*. Cambridge: Polity.

George, M. (2014) 'Rejecting the Specifically Sexual: Locating the Sexual Field in the Work of Pierre Bourdieu', in I. Green (Ed.) *Sexual Fields*. Chicago, IL: University of Chicago Press, pp. 101–22.

Gerbner, G. and Gross, L. (1976) 'Living with Television'. *Journal of Communication*, 26 (2): 172–94.

Giddens, A. (1984) *The Constitution of Society*. Cambridge: Polity.

Giddens, A. (1992) *The Transformation of Intimacy*. Cambridge: Polity.

Giddens, A. (1998) *The Third Way*. Cambridge: Polity.

Gillies, V. (2006) 'Working Class Mothers and School Life: Exploring the Role of Emotional Capital'. *Gender and Education*, 18 (3), 281–93.

Gillies, V. (2007) *Marginalised Mothers*. London: Routledge.

Gillis, J. (1996) *A World of Their Own Making*. Cambridge, MA: Harvard University Press.

Go, J. (2008) 'Global Fields and Imperial Forms'. *Sociological Theory*, 26 (3): 201–29.

Goffman, E. (1976) *Gender Advertisements*. London: Macmillan.

Goldberg-Hiller, J. (2004) *The Limits to Union*. Ann Arbor, MI: University of Michigan Press.

Goldthorpe, J.H. (2007) ' "Cultural Capital": Some Critical Observations', *Sociologica*, 2: DOI: 10.2383/24755.

Goodman, J. and Silverstein, P. (Eds.) (2009) *Bourdieu in Algeria*. Lincoln, NE: University of Nebraska Press.

Gopnik, A., Meltzoff, A. and Kuhl, P. (1999) *How Babies Think*. London: Weidenfeld and Nicolson.

Green, I. (2008) 'The Social Organization of Desire'. *Sociological Theory*, 26 (1): 25–50.

Green, I. (2014) 'The Sexual Fields Framework', in I. Green (Ed.) *Sexual Fields*. Chicago, IL: University of Chicago Press, pp. 25–56.

Grenfell, M. (2010) 'Working with *Habitus* and *Field*', in E. Silva and A. Warde (Eds.) *Cultural Analysis and Bourdieu's Legacy*. London: Routledge, pp. 14–27.

Grieshaber, S. (2004) *Rethinking Parent and Child Conflict*. New York: RoutledgeFalmer.

Hage, G. (1998) *White Nation: Fantasies of White Supremacy in a Multicultural Society*. London: Routledge.

Hägerstrand, T. (1967) *Innovation Diffusion as a Spatial Process*. Chicago, IL: University of Chicago Press.

Hägerstrand, T. (1975) 'Space, Time and Human Conditions', in A. Karlqvist (Ed.) *Dynamic Allocation of Urban Space*. Farnborough: Saxon House, pp. 3–14.

Haith, M. (1980) *Rules that Babies Look By*. Hillsdale, NJ: Erlbaum.

Hakim, C. (2000) *Work-Lifestyle Choices in the 21st Century*. Oxford: Oxford University Press.

Hakim, C. (2012) *Honey Money*. London: Penguin.

Hall, S. (1980) 'Encoding/Decoding', in S. Hall, D. Hobson, A. Lowe and P. Willis (Eds.) *Culture, Media, Language*. London: Hutchinson, pp. 128–38.

Hartup, W. (1998) 'The Company They Keep', in A. Campbell and S. Muncer (Eds.) *The Social Child*. Hove: Psychology Press, pp. 143–64.

Harvey, D. (1989) *The Condition of Postmodernity*. Oxford: Blackwell.

Heller, A. (1984) *Everyday Life*. London: Routledge and Kegan Paul.

Hilgers, M. and Mangez, E. (Eds.) (2014) *Bourdieu's Theory of Social Fields: Concepts and Applications*. London: Routledge.

Hillier, J. and Rooksby, E. (Eds.) (2005) *Habitus: A Sense of Place* (2nd edn). Aldershot: Ashgate.

Hochschild, A. (1989) *The Second Shift*. New York: Viking.

Holt, D.B. (1997) 'Distinction in America? Recovering Bourdieu's Theory of Tastes from its Critics'. *Poetics*, 25 (2): 93–120.

Honneth, A. (1986) 'The Fragmented World of Symbolic Forms: Reflections on Pierre Bourdieu's Sociology'. *Theory, Culture and Society*, 3 (1): 55–66.

Honneth, A. (1996) *The Struggle for Recognition*. Cambridge: Polity.

Howes, C. (1998) 'The Earliest Friendships', in W. Bukowski, A. Newcomb and W. Hartup (Eds.) *The Company They Keep*. Cambridge: Cambridge University Press, pp. 66–86.

Huppatz, K. (2009) 'Reworking Bourdieu's "Capital"'. *Sociology*, 43 (1): 45–66.

Husserl, E. (1992) *The Phenomenology of Internal Time Consciousness*. Dordrecht: Kluwer.

Husserl, E. (2001) *Analyses Concerning Active and Passive Synthesis*. The Hague: Martinus Nijhoff.

Illouz, E. (1997) 'Who Will Care for the Caretaker's Daughter?'. *Theory, Culture and Society*, 14 (4): 31–66.

Illouz, E. (2012) *Why Love Hurts*. Cambridge: Polity.

Ingram, N. (2011) 'Within School and Beyond the Gate'. *Sociology*, 45 (2): 287–302.

Irwin, S. and Elley, S. (2013) 'Parents' Hopes and Expectations for Their Children's Future Occupations'. *The Sociological Review*, 61 (1): 111–30.

Jaeger, M. and Breen, R. (2013) *A Dynamic Model of Cultural Reproduction*. Working Paper No. 03/2013, The Danish Centre for Social Research, Copenhagen.

James, A. (2013) *Socialising Children*. Basingstoke: Palgrave Macmillan.

James, A. and Prout, A. (Eds.) (1990) *Constructing and Reconstructing Childhood*. London: Falmer.

James, A. and Prout, A. (1996) 'Strategies and Structures: Towards a New Perspective on Children's Experiences of Family Life', in J. Brannen and M. O'Brien (Eds.) *Children in Families*. London: Falmer, pp. 41–52.

James, W. (1950) *The Principles of Psychology* (Vol. 1). New York: Dover.

Jameson, F. (1991) *Postmodernism, or, the Cultural Logic of Late Capitalism*. London: Verso.

Jamieson, L. (1998) *Intimacy*. Cambridge: Polity.

Jarness, V. (2013) 'Class, Status, Closure: The Petropolis and Cultural Life'. Unpublished PhD thesis, University of Bergen, Norway.

Jenkins, R. (2002) *Pierre Bourdieu* (2nd edn). London: Routledge.

Jung, C. (1961) *Freud and Psychoanalysis*. London: Routledge and Kegan Paul.

Jung, C. (1969) *The Structure and Dynamics of the Psyche*. London: Routledge and Kegan Paul.

Kaufmann, J.C. (2009) *Gripes: The Little Quarrels of Couples*. Cambridge: Polity.

Kaufmann, V. (2002) *Re-thinking Mobility*. Aldershot: Ashgate.

Kaufmann, V. (2011) *Rethinking the City*. London: Routledge.

Kaufmann, V., Bergman, M. and Joye, D. (2004) 'Motility: Mobility as Capital'. *International Journal of Urban and Regional Research*, 28 (4): 745–56.

Kessler, S. and McKenna, W. (1978) *Gender: An Ethnomethodological Approach*. Chicago, IL: University of Chicago Press.

Kisilevsky, B.S., Hains, S.M., Lee, K., Xie, X., Huang, H., Ye, H.H., Zhang, K. and Wang, Z. (2003) 'Effects of Experience on Fetal Voice Recognition'. *Psychological Science*, 14 (3): 220–4.

Kitchener, R. (1991) 'Jean Piaget: The Unknown Sociologist?'. *British Journal of Sociology*, 42 (3): 421–42.

Klein, M. (1932) *The Psychoanalysis of Children*. London: Hogarth Press.

Kojève, A. (1969) *Introduction to the Reading of Hegel: Lectures on the 'Phenomenology of Spirit'* (trans. J.H. Nichols). Ithaca, NY: Cornell University Press.

Krais, B. (1993) 'Gender and Symbolic Violence', in C. Calhoun, E. LiPuma and M. Postone (Eds.) *Bourdieu: Critical Perspectives*. Cambridge: Polity, pp. 156–77.

Krais, B. (2006) 'Gender, Sociological Theory and Bourdieu's Sociology of Practice'. *Theory, Culture and Society*, 23 (6): 119–34.

Kuhn, S. and Stiner, M. (2006) 'What's a Mother to Do? The Division of Labour among Neanderthals and Modern Humans in Eurasia'. *Current Anthropology*, 47 (6): 953–81.

Lacan, J. (1977/2001) *Écrits: A Selection*. London: Routledge.

Lahire, B. (1998) 'Champ, Hors-champ, Contrechamp', in B. Lahire (Ed.) *Le Travail Sociologique de Pierre Bourdieu*. Paris: La Découverte, pp. 23–58.

Lahire, B. (2002) *Portraits Sociologique*. Paris: Armand.

Lahire, B. (2003) 'From the Habitus to an Individual Heritage of Dispositions'. *Poetics*, 31 (5): 329–55.

Lahire, B. (2011) *The Plural Actor*. Cambridge: Polity.

Laing, R.D. (1971) *The Politics of the Family and Other Essays*. London: Tavistock.

Lane, J. (2000) *Pierre Bourdieu: A Critical Introduction*. London: Pluto Press.

Lane, J. (2006) *Bourdieu's Politics*. London: Routledge.

Lareau, A. (2000) *Home Advantage* (2nd edn). Lanham, MD: Rowman and Littlefield.

Lareau, A. (2003) *Unequal Childhoods*. Berkeley, CA: University of California Press.

Laqueur, T. (1990) *Making Sex: Body and Gender from the Greeks to Freud*. Cambridge, MA: Harvard University Press.

Latour, B. (2005) *Reassembling the Social*. Oxford: Oxford University Press.

Lawler, S. (2000) *Mothering the Self*. London: Routledge.

Layder, D. (2006) *Understanding Social Theory* (2nd edn). London: Sage.

Lemke, T. (2015) 'New Materialisms: Foucault and the "Government of Things" '. *Theory, Culture and Society*, 32 (4): 3–25.

Lenntorp, B. (1976) *Paths in Space-Time Environments: A Time Geographic Study of Movement Possibilities of Individuals*. Lund Studies in Geography, Series B: Human Geography. Lund: Gleerup.

Lenntorp, B. (1999) 'Time-Geography – at the End of its Beginning'. *GeoJournal*, 48 (3): 155–8.

Lenoir, R. (2003) *Généalogie de la Morale Familiale*. Paris: Seuil.

Lévi-Strauss, C. (1969) *The Elementary Structures of Kinship*. Boston, MA: Beacon Press.

Lizardo, O. (2004) 'The Cognitive Origins of Bourdieu's *Habitus*'. *Journal for the Theory of Social Behaviour*, 34 (4): 375–401.

Lizardo, O. (2006) 'How Cultural Tastes Shape Personal Networks'. *American Sociological Review*, 71 (5): 778–807.

Lloyd, B. (1987) 'Social Representations of Gender', in J. Bruner and H. Haste (Eds.) *Making Sense: The Child's Construction of the World*. London: Methuen, pp. 147–62.

Lovell, T. (2000) 'Thinking Feminism With and Against Bourdieu'. *Feminist Theory*, 1 (1): 11–32.

Lovell, T. (2004) 'Bourdieu, Class and Feminism', in L. Adkins and B. Skeggs (Eds.) *Feminism After Bourdieu*. Oxford: Blackwell, pp. 37–56.

Mac an Ghaill, M. (1994) *The Making of Men*. Buckingham: Open University Press.

Mann, M. (1986) *The Sources of Social Power, Volume 1*. Cambridge: Cambridge University Press.

Mannheim, K. (1952) *Essays on the Sociology of Knowledge*. London: Routledge and Kegan Paul.

Martin, J.L. and George, M. (2006) 'Theories of Sexual Stratification'. *Sociological Theory*, 24 (2): 107–32.

Marx, K. (1956) *Capital* (Vol. 2). London: Lawrence and Wishart.

Mauss, M. (1954/2002) *The Gift*. London: Routledge.

McCall, L. (1992) 'Does Gender Fit?'. *Theory and Society*, 21 (6): 837–67.

McKibbin, R. (1998) *Classes and Cultures: England 1918–51*. Oxford: Oxford University Press.

McNay, L. (1999) 'Gender, Habitus and the Field'. *Theory, Culture and Society*, 16 (1): 95–117.

McNay, L. (2008) *Against Recognition*. Cambridge: Polity.

McPherson, M., Smith-Lovin, L. and Cook, J. (2001) 'Birds of a Feather: Homophily in Social Networks'. *Annual Review of Sociology*, 27: 415–44.

McRae, S. (1986) *Cross-Class Families*. Oxford: Clarendon Press.

Mead, G.H. (1934) *Mind, Self and Society*. Chicago, IL: University of Chicago Press.

Meltzoff, A. and Moore, M. (1977) 'Imitation of Facial and Manual Gestures by Human Neonates'. *Science*, 198 (4312): 75–8.

Merleau-Ponty, M. (2002) *Phenomenology of Perception*. London: Routledge.

Merleau-Ponty, M. (2014) *Child Psychology and Pedagogy*. Evanston, IL: Northwestern University Press.

Miller, D.L. (2014) 'Symbolic Capital and Gender'. *Cultural Sociology*, 8 (4): 462–82.

Mitchell, J. (2003) *Siblings*. Cambridge: Polity.

Moi, T. (1991) 'Appropriating Bourdieu'. *New Literary History*, 22 (4): 1017–49.

Morgan, D. (1996) *Family Connections*. Cambridge: Polity.

Morgan, D. (1999) 'Risk and Family Practices', in E.B. Silva and C. Smart (Eds.) *The New Family?* London: Sage, pp. 13–30.

Morgan, D. (2011) *Rethinking Family Practices*. Basingstoke: Palgrave Macmillan.

Mottier, V. (2002) 'Masculine Domination'. *Feminist Theory*, 3 (3): 345–59.

Mouzelis, N. (1995) *Social Theory: What Went Wrong?* London: Routledge.

Nooy, W. de (2003) 'Fields and Networks'. *Poetics*, 31 (5–6): 305–27.

Nowotny, H. (1981) 'Women in Public Life in Austria', in C.F. Epstein and R.L. Coser (Eds.) *Access to Power: Cross-National Studies of Women and Elites*. London: Allen & Unwin.

Oakley, A. (1976) *Housewife*. Harmondsworth: Penguin.

O'Brien, M., Alldred, P. and Jones, D. (1996) 'Children's Constructions of Family and Kinship', in J. Brannen and M. O'Brien (Eds.) *Children in Families*. London: Falmer, pp. 84–100.

O'Connell, R. (2010) '(How) is Childminding Family Like? Family Day Care, Food and the Reproduction of Identity at the Public/Private Interface'. *The Sociological Review*, 58 (4): 563–86.

Office for National Statistics (2010) *Social Trends No. 40*. Basingstoke: Palgrave.

Ohnmacht, T., Maksi, H. and Bergman, M. (Eds.) (2009) *Mobilities and Inequality*. Farnham: Ashgate.

Pahl, J. (1989) *Money and Marriage*. London: Macmillan.

Painter, J. (2000) 'Pierre Bourdieu', in M. Crang and N. Thrift (Eds.) *Thinking Space*. London: Routledge, pp. 239–59.

Parsons, T. and Bales, R. (1956) *Family Socialization and Interaction Process*. London: Routledge and Kegan Paul.

Perrier, M. (2010) 'Developing the "Right" Kind of Child: Younger and Older Mothers' Classed Moral Projects', in M. Klett-Davies (Ed.) *Is Parenting a Class Issue?* London: Family and Parenting Institute, pp. 17–30.

Phillips, R. (1991) *Untying the Knot*. Cambridge: Cambridge University Press.

Piaget, J. (1932) *The Moral Judgement of the Child*. Glencoe, IL: The Free Press.

Piaget, J. (1962) *Play, Dreams and Imitation in Childhood*. New York: W. W. Norton.

Piaget, J. (1972) 'Intellectual Evolution from Adolescence to Adulthood'. *Human Development*, 15 (1): 1–12.

Piaget, J. (1977) *The Origin of Intelligence in the Child*. Harmondsworth: Penguin.

Piaget, J. and Inhelder, B. (1969) *The Psychology of the Child*. London: Routledge and Kegan Paul.

Porter, R.H. and Winburg, J. (1999) 'Unique Salience of Maternal Breast Odors for Newborn Infants'. *Neuroscience & Biobehavioural Reviews*, 23 (3): 439–49.

Powell, C. and Dépelteau, F. (Eds.) (2013) *Conceptualizing Relational Sociology*. Basingstoke: Palgrave Macmillan.

Pred, A. (1977) 'The Choreography of Existence'. *Economic Geography*, 53 (2): 207–21.

Pred, A. (1981a) 'Social Reproduction and the Time-Geography of Everyday Life'. *Geografiska Annaler, Series B, Human Geography*, 63 (1): 5–22.

Pred, A. (1981b) 'Power, Everyday Practice and the Discipline of Human Geography', in A. Pred (Ed.) *Space and Time in Geography*. Lund: CWK Gleerup, pp. 30–55.

Prieur, A., Rosenlund, L. and Skjott-Larsen, J. (2008) 'Cultural Capital Today: A Case Study from Denmark'. *Poetics*, 36 (1): 45–71.

Rancière, J. (2004) *The Philosopher and His Poor*. London: Duke University Press.

Reay, D. (1998) *Class Work*. London: UCL Press.

Reay, D. (2000) 'A Useful Extension of Bourdieu's Conceptual Framework?'. *Sociological Review*, 48 (4): 568–85.

Reay, D. (2004) 'Gendering Bourdieu's Concepts of Capitals? Emotional Capital, Women and Social Class'. *The Sociological Review*, 52 (s2): 57–74.

Reay, D. (2005) 'Beyond Consciousness? The Psychic Landscape of Social Class'. *Sociology*, 39 (5): 911–28.

Reay, D. and Lucey, H. (2002) ' "I Don't Really Like it Here But I Don't Want to Be Anywhere Else": Children and Inner City Council Estates'. *Antipode*, 32 (4): 410–28.

Reay, D., David, M. and Ball, S. (2005) *Degrees of Choice*. Stoke-on-Trent: Trentham.

Reay, D., Crozier, G. and James, D. (2011) *White Middle-Class Identities and Urban Schooling*. Basingstoke: Palgrave Macmillan.

Ribbens, J. (1994) *Mothers and Their Children*. London: Sage.

Rose, N. (1999) *Powers of Freedom: Reframing Political Thought*. Cambridge: Cambridge University Press.

Roseneil, S. (2006) 'On Not Living with a Partner: Unpicking Coupledom and Cohabitation'. *Sociological Research Online*, 11 (3).

Rosenlund, L. (2009) *Exploring the City with Bourdieu*. Saarbrücken: VDM Verlag.

Rubin, G. (1975) 'The Traffic in Women', in R. Reiter (Ed.) *Toward an Anthropology of Women*. London: Monthly Review Press, pp. 157–210.

Rubin, K., Lynch, D., Coplan, R., Rose-Krasnor, L. and Booth, C. (1994) ' "Birds of a Feather ...": Behavioral Concordances and Preferential Personal Attraction in Children'. *Child Development*, 65 (6): 1778–85.

Sales, A. (2012) 'Reconsidering Processes of Reproduction Through Learning'. Unpublished PhD Thesis, University of Sheffield.

Savage, M. (2010) The Politics of Elective Belonging. *Housing, Theory and Society*, 27 (2): 115–61.

Savage, M. (2011) 'The Lost Urban Sociology of Pierre Bourdieu', in G. Bridge and S. Watson (Eds.) *The New Blackwell Companion to the City.* Oxford: Blackwell, pp. 511–20.

Savage, M., Bagnall, G. and Longhurst, B. (2005) *Globalization and Belonging.* London: Sage.

Sayad, A. (2004) *The Suffering of the Immigrant.* Cambridge: Polity.

Sayer, A. (2005) *The Moral Significance of Class.* Cambridge: Cambridge University Press.

Schliemann, A. and Nunes, T. (1990) 'A Situated Schema of Proportionality'. *British Journal of Developmental Psychology,* 8 (3): 259–68.

Schutz, A. (1970) *Reflections on the Problem of Relevance.* New Haven, CT: Yale University Press.

Schutz, A. (1972) *The Phenomenology of the Social World.* Evanston, IL: Northwestern University Press.

Schutz, A. and Luckmann, T. (1973) *The Structure of the Life-World* (Vol. 1). Evanston, IL: Northwestern University Press.

Seamon, D. (1979) *A Geography of the Lifeworld: Movement, Rest and Encounter.* London: Croom Helm.

Shilling, C. (2003) *The Body and Social Theory* (2nd edn). London: Sage.

Shorter, E. (1976) *The Making of the Modern Family.* London: Collins.

Silva, E.B. (2005) 'Gender, Home and Family in Cultural Capital Theory'. *British Journal of Sociology,* 56 (1): 83–103.

Silva, E.B. (2010) *Technology, Culture, Family.* Basingstoke: Palgrave Macmillan.

Silva, E.B. (2016) 'Unity and Fragmentation of the Habitus'. *The Sociological Review,* DOI: 10.1111/1467-954X.12346.

Siraj, I. and Mayo, A. (2014) *Social Class and Educational Inequality: The Impact of Parents and Schools.* Cambridge: Cambridge University Press.

Skeggs, B. (1997) *Formations of Class and Gender.* London: Sage.

Skeggs, B. (2004) 'Context and Background: Pierre Bourdieu's Analysis of Class, Gender and Sexuality', in L. Adkins and B. Skeggs (Eds.) *Feminism After Bourdieu.* Oxford: Blackwell, pp. 19–33.

Smart, C. (2007) *Personal Life.* Cambridge: Polity.

Smart, C., Neale, B. and Wade, A. (2001) *The Changing Experience of Childhood.* Cambridge: Polity.

Smith, D. (1987) *The Everyday World as Problematic*. Boston, MA: Northwestern University Press.

Smith, D. (1990) *The Conceptual Practices of Power*. Boston, MA: Northwestern University Press.

Stahl, G. (2015) *Identity, Neoliberalism and Aspiration*. London: Routledge.

Steinbock, A.J. (1995) *Home and Beyond: Generative Phenomenology After Husserl*. Evanston, IL: Northwestern University Press.

Steinmetz, G. (2006) 'Bourdieu's Disavowal of Lacan'. *Constellations*, 13 (4): 445–64.

Steinmetz, G. (2014) 'From Sociology to Socioanalysis', in L. Chancer and J. Andrews (Eds.) *The Unhappy Divorce of Sociology and Psychoanalysis*. Basingstoke: Palgrave Macmillan, pp. 203–19.

Swartz, D. (1997) *Culture and Power*. Chicago, IL: University of Chicago Press.

Swartz, D. (2013) 'Metaprinciples for Sociological Research in a Bourdieusian Perspective', in P. Gorski (Ed.) *Bourdieu and Historical Analysis*. Durham, NC: Duke University Press, pp. 19–35.

Therborn, G. (2004) *Between Sex and Power: Family in the World, 1900–2000*. London: Routledge.

Thompson, J. (1995) *The Media and Modernity*. Cambridge: Polity.

Thrift, N. (1981) 'Owners' Time and Own Time: the Making of a Capitalist Time-Consciousness, 1300–1880', in A. Pred (Ed.) *Space and Time in Geography*. Lund: CWK Gleerup, pp. 56–84.

Thrift, N. (1996) *Spatial Formations*. London: Sage.

Tizard, B. and Hughes, M. (2002) *Young Children Learning* (2nd edn). Oxford: Blackwell.

Trevarthen, C. and Aitken, K. (2001) 'Infant Intersubjectivity'. *Journal of Child Psychology and Psychiatry*, 42 (1): 3–48.

Tuma, N. and Hallinan, M. (1979) 'The Effects of Sex, Race and Achievement on Schoolchildren's Friendships'. *Social Forces*, 57 (4): 1265–85.

Urry, J. (2007) *Mobilities*. Cambridge: Polity.

Vandebroeck, D. (forthcoming) *Distinctions in the Flesh*. London: Routledge.

Vandenberghe, F. (1999) ' "The Real is Relational": An Epistemological Analysis of Pierre Bourdieu's Generative Structuralism'. *Sociological Theory*, 17 (1): 32–67.

Vygotsky, L. (1978) *Mind in Society*. Cambridge, MA: Harvard University Press.

Vygotsky, L. (2012) *Thought and Language*. Cambridge, MA: MIT Press.

Wacquant, L. (1989) 'Social Ontology, Epistemology, and Class'. *Berkeley Journal of Sociology*, 34: 165–86.

Wacquant, L. (1993) 'Bourdieu in America', in C. Calhoun, E. LiPuma and M. Postone (Eds.) *Bourdieu: Critical Perspectives*. Cambridge: Polity, pp. 235–62.

Wacquant, L. (1995) 'Pugs at Work: Bodily Capital and Bodily Labour among Professional Boxers'. *Body and Society*, 1 (1): 65–93.

Wacquant, L. (2004) *Body and Soul*. Oxford: Oxford University Press.

Wacquant, L. (2009) *Punishing the Poor*. Durham, NC: Duke University Press.

Wacquant, L. (2014) 'Putting Habitus in its Place'. *Body and Society*, 20 (2): 118–39.

Walby, S. (1997) *Gender Transformations*. London: Routledge.

Walker, K.N. and Messinger, L. (1979) 'Remarriage after Divorce: Dissolution and Reconstruction of Family Boundaries'. *Family Process*, 18 (2): 185–92.

Walkerdine, V. (1984) 'Developmental Psychology and the Child-Centred Pedagogy', in J. Henriques, W. Hollway, C. Urwin, C. Venn and V. Walkerdine, *Changing the Subject*. London: Methuen, pp. 153–202.

Walkerdine, V. and Lucey, H. (1989) *Democracy in the Kitchen*. London: Virago.

Weeks, J. (1991) 'Pretended Family Relationships', in D. Clark (Ed.) *Marriage, Domestic Life and Social Change*. London: Routledge, pp. 214–34.

Weeks, J. (2007) *The World We Have Won*. London: Routledge.

Welsh, T. (2013) *The Child as Natural Phenomenologist*. Evanston, IL: Northwestern University Press.

West, C. and Zimmerman, D. (1987) 'Doing Gender'. *Gender and Society*, 1 (2): 125–51.

Widmer, E.D. (2010) *Family Configurations*. London: Ashgate.

Wiley, N. (1985) 'Marriage and the Construction of Reality: Then and Now', in G. Handel (Ed.) *The Psychosocial Interior of the Family* (3rd edn). New York: Aldine de Gruyter, pp. 21–32.

Williams, R. (1983) *Keywords* (2nd edn). London: Flamingo.

Willis, P. (1977) *Learning to Labour*. Farnborough: Saxon House.

Witz, A. (2004) 'Anamnesis and Amnesis in Bourdieu's Work', in L. Adkins and B. Skeggs (Eds.) *Feminism After Bourdieu*. Oxford: Blackwell, pp. 211–23.

Wright, E.O. (2001) 'A Conceptual Menu for Studying the Interconnections of Class and Gender', in J. Baxter and M. Western (Eds.) *Reconfigurations of Class and Gender*. Stanford, CA: Stanford University Press, pp. 28–38.

Yorke, B. (1990) *Kings and Kingdoms in Early Anglo-Saxon England*. London: Seaby.

Index

Facebook *see* social media
Fairbairn, R. 76
family 7–8, 9, 12, 42, 43–5,
    45–6, 71, 73, 83, 90,
    91–2, 97–8, 99, 121, 123,
    124, 125, 129, 130
  boundaries 66–9, 145n4
  doxa 51–7, 67, 68, 69, 84,
    85, 94, 96, 98, 100, 101,
    102, 145n2
  field 12, 15, 25, 31, 34, 35,
    37, 57–66, 67, 68–70, 71,
    71, 82, 84–6, 92–3,
    94–6, 97, 98, 100, 101,
    102, 103, 115, 118, 125,
    127, 128, 130, 131,
    132–3, 135–6, 138, 140,
    141, 145n2, 145n4,
    145n5, 147n7
  realization 49–51, 69
  symbolic struggle
    over 46–9, 69, 112,
    145n1
  see also Bourdieu, P., on
    family
family practice theory 57,
    145n2
feminism 9, 43, 104–6, 108,
    111, 112, 114, 123,
    127–8, 138
field
  analysis 10, 13–14, 41,
    141–2
  artistic 34, 52, 111, 144n3
  bureaucratic 18, 32, 33, 36,
    111, 124, 132, 139
  and circuits of symbolic
    power 31–7, 139, 141
  of cultural production 18,
    47, 63, 66, 67, 88, 93,
    125, 131

economic 15, 18, 26, 35,
    47, 50, 64, 88, 124, 125,
    131, 135, 144n3, 144n5
family *see* family, field
of gender 9, 104, 106, 115,
    119
and habitus 2, 72, 74,
    82–3, 146n1
intellectual 3, 25, 26, 28,
    51, 112, 135, 136, 144n3,
    146n1
legal 32, 33, 111
media 18, 28, 32, 34, 36,
    48, 98, 111, 113, 118
medical 82, 141
military 125, 141
misuse of 3
and networks/time-space
    6–8, 16–19, 27–31,
    39–42
political 15, 32, 37, 47, 48,
    111, 112, 132, 135
of power 7, 14, 15, 26, 33,
    34, 35, 36, 39, 47–9, 50,
    51, 69, 98, 111–14, 118,
    123–4, 127, 131, 132,
    135, 136, 137, 138, 141,
    142
religious 48, 50, 111
scientific 10, 35, 111, 132,
    137, 148n2
sexual 93, 116–20, 126,
    138, 141
sociological 2, 68, 146n1
of sport 29, 118, 125
see also epistemic and
    empirical individuals;
    family, as field; micro-
    fields; multiplicity; social
    space; social surface
Foucault, M. 34, 44, 50